© 1999
Ventajas, L.L.C.
6547 Sperryville Pike
Boston, Virginia 22713
www.SocialWorkInfo.com

INTRODUCTION

■ People learn in different ways. Sometimes, a short, sweet fact or a familiar concept is a perfect stimulus for thought. This little volume is meant to get you thinking, remembering, and studying those things that will help you with your licensure examinations. It can be used in other connections as well. If your prefer short stories to novels, this approach will appeal to you! Take this handy volume with you, and when you have a spare moment during the day, pull it out and read a little.

■ Test question writers are known for creating complex and lengthy items, full of details that can confuse test takers. The item writers can't change the realities of the facts and concepts, however.

■ The facts, concepts, and definitions in this handy volume are all important to know. You may well meet some of them on your examination!

■ If you enjoy this book and want to put some energy into learning the skills of multiple choice test taking, you may want to dig deeper by studying one of our Licensure Examination Study Manuals. You can order them from our website at www.SocialWorkInfo.com or by using the order form at the end of this book.

■ Whatever your choices, good luck!

Eli and Frances

- **Drug abuse** is recurrent drug use that results in disruption of academic, social, and occupational functioning, or in legal or psychological problems.

- **Service accessibility** is generally considered to be the location — in a neighborhood, community, or state — of social or human agencies sensitive to the delivery of services needed by a particular clientele.

- **Professional accountability** is the requirement to respond and provide services in such a manner that clients are assured that high levels of standards are met.

- **Accrediting** of agencies and programs supported by those agencies is a voluntary activity used to determine to what degree an agency meets or exceeds standards.

- Completion of a predetermined treatment/services regimen, with no further treatment services prescribed, is known as **achieved treatment or service goals**.

- **Action research**, a research design typically used for planning and community organization, includes data collection with the purpose of directly dealing with a social problem through development and implementation of services programs.

- The term **acute** pertains to intense conditions or disturbances of relatively short duration.

- Mental disorders lasting under six months are considered to be acute; those lasting more than six months are termed **chronic**.

- **Acute care** is a set of health, personal, or social services delivered to individuals who require short-term assistance. Acute care is usually provided in hospitals or community social agencies where the extended treatment of long-term care is not expected.

- **Addiction** is a physiological or psychological dependence on a chemical resulting in increased tolerance and in withdrawal symptoms when the substance is unavailable.

- **Addictive substances** include alcohol, tobacco, narcotics, and many sedative drugs.

- **Social work administration** is a coordinated effort in an organization to develop, implement, and evaluate policies and procedures in a services delivery system.

- **Administrative and support staff** in social work programs typically includes managers and administrators, office assistants, secretaries, computer programmers/analysts, evaluation specialists, researchers, and security officers.

- **Administrative staff** includes personnel responsible for the administration or management of staff to achieve predetermined organizational/agency goals and objectives.

- Contents of a **client, or clinical, record** include demographic and clinical data collected for the purpose of making decisions regarding admission, treatment regimen, interventions, and intervention implementation. Generally, a clinical record includes the following: client's name, address, telephone number, date of birth, sex, race/ethnic origin, presenting problem, date of initial interview or intake date and location of last treatment episode, referral source, and recommendations for aftercare services.

- Post-discharge activities offered on an as-needed basis and geared to assist the client maintain or improve on the progress made during treatment are defined as *aftercare.*

- **Aftercare services** are not typically part of any case management responsibility for the client — and it is essentially the client who initiates contact with the program — but they may serve as a means for relapse prevention and determining a client's status.

- **Acquired Immune Deficiency Syndrome (AIDS)** is a viral disease, usually fatal, that prevents the body's immune system from functioning. The AIDS virus is transmitted through exchanges of body fluids such as infected blood or semen. Individuals infected with the AIDS virus tend to become ill with a variety of illnesses such as pneumonia or cancer.

- **Alcohol and drug histories** provide details regarding psychoactive drugs and alcohol used in the past; preferred drugs; frequency of use; route of administration; age and year of first use of alcohol and each drug; previous experience with overdose, withdrawal, adverse drug reactions; and attempts at alcohol/drug abuse treatment.

- **Alcoholism** is a physical and at times a psychological dependence on the consumption of alcohol which may lead to social, mental, or physical impairment.

- **Amphetamine**, a drug that stimulates the cerebral cortex, tends to increase one's mental alertness temporarily. Amphetamine, known on the street as "bennies," "uppers," and "speed," is addictive and requires increased doses as tolerance develops.

- **Angel dust** is a street term for the psychedelic or hallucinogenic drug PCP (phencyclidine).

- **Antabuse** is a regulated drug which induces nausea when taken with alcohol which and is experienced as aversive by individuals who use alcohol.

- **Applied research** is a research design used in the study of social and psychological phenomena or dynamics and in finding solutions to immediate social and psychological problems.

- Social Workers consider an **appointment** to be an agreed upon and dedicated period of time for the delivery and reception of services, usually lasting 50 minutes to one hour for individuals and couples and 90 to 120 minutes for groups.

- **Assessment** is a data collection and analysis process used to determine the nature, cause, and progression of a problem. Assessment is fundamental to treatment plan development, and information acquired during this process is useful in the identification and selection of treatment models and interventions. Assessment can also assist in the determination of a client's strengths and weaknesses and may influence the treatment process.

- **At-risk clients** are individuals who are vulnerable to or may be adversely affected by a social, psychological, or environmental circumstance.

- **Service audits** are global inspections and assessments of services or clinical records of an individual or organization. Service audits are most often used to verify clinical or organization services and the various processes used in the delivery of services or meeting organizational mission.

- **Barbiturates**, drugs that act the central nervous system, are often used to assist in sleep or to control convulsive disorders.

- In community practice, **bargaining** includes the negotiation of agreements between various groups or stockholders to ensure the all parties share in resources, activities, and outcomes.

- **Baseline** is a term used by social research or mental health providers who are interested in the documentation of the frequency with which behaviors occur. Baseline data is usually acquired before any interventions are imposed to deal with behavior.

- **Bias** is a preestablished value, belief, or attitude which influences emotions or thoughts and which can result in an individual's having a positive or negative predisposition about a particular person, object, group, individual, or behavior.

- **Statistical bias** is a tendency for findings to lean in a particular direction.

- A group of community leaders with the power and influence to develop and evaluate a particular organization's policies and procedure is typically referred to as a **board of directors**.

- **Brainstorming** is an activity in which ideas are generated from staff, consultants, and administrators through the use of an open discussion with controls on both criticism or examination of ideas presented.

- A **budget** is a management tool used by organizational staff, listing all revenues and the use of the revenues in the day-to-day operations of the organization.

- A **care giver** is a services provider who attempts to meet the physical, emotional, and social needs of another person.

- **Case finding** is the process of identifying individuals or groups who are in need of a specific service or who are vulnerable to social or psychological situational circumstances.

- The purpose of **case management** is to coordinate services on behalf of a client or group of clients. Case management allows for a number of Social Workers within an organization to organize and manage varied resources with the goal of providing the most effective and efficient services. Case management may include the day-to-day monitoring of client progress, continued assessment, and case consultation. Case management is a fundamental social work activity which discourages the duplication of services and service fragmentation by auditing services provided to clients.

- **Case integration** is a process which involves the management of social work activities and service providers from other disciplines who are simultaneously serving the needs of a client or client group. Case integration usually involves the delivery of services which are consistent, non-duplicative, and directed toward achieving similar treatment or services goals and objectives.

- A **case conference** is an activity used in social agencies to coordinate treatment or services. Social Workers, along with administrative staff, discuss and review a client's problem, treatment objectives, and intervention plans. Case conferences usually involve professionals from a variety of disciplines, consultants, and client's relatives who are sensitive to the client's needs or responsible for the provision of a direct service to the client. Participants in a case conference may include the Social Workers who are providing the direct service to the client or client system and the professional supervisor of these workers.

- **Case study** is the collection and study of data directed toward the systematic evaluation of many variables specific to a case.

- A *caseload* is the assigned set of cases for which a social work is responsible. An active caseload is generally about 45 clients, although some assignments are as high as 100.

- A *catchment area* is a predetermined geographic region, neighborhood, or community in which potential clients are served by a designated social agency.

- *Certification* of a profession typically occurs as result of legislation which requires that a certified individual has attained a specified level of formal training, experiences, and/or skills.

- *Change agents* are helping professionals, including Social Workers, who are interested in the delivery of specific or specialized services to a client or client group in need of the services.

- *Chemotherapy* is a form of treatment which uses chemicals for dealing with cognitive, emotional, and interpersonal problems.

- A *chronic condition* is persistent medical problem or condition that is likely to restrict or prevent full use of an individual's physical, psychological, or social functioning abilities.

- In *community practice* many Social Workers work closely with various types of citizen participation groups, including social agencies.

- *Active cases* are individuals, groups, families, communities, or agencies, who have been admitted, approved, or accepted for case management activities and advocacy activities, for whom a treatment/service plan has been developed, who have received scheduled services for at least once a month, and who have not been discharged from treatment/services.

- *Client rights* include knowing existing health care alternatives and providers of the alternatives. Client rights include the client's informed participation in all decisions involving health care, respect for privacy, clear explanation of all interventions (including risk of death or side effects), clear and accurate evaluation of condition and prognosis before inter-

ventions, access to information contained in clinical record, freedom to refuse any treatment, and freedom to terminate services.

- An **active client** is an individual who has been accepted, admitted, or approved for social work services, who has an open client treatment record, who has had an initial first face-to-face treatment/service contact from a social work professional, and who has received at least one face-to-face treatment/service contact every 30 days from a social work professional.

- Generally, a **client** is defined as an individual (or group of individuals) who has a personal problem, has been admitted or approved for treatment, and is receiving treatment/recovery service for a mental health related problem.

- **Client system** may be an individual, family, group, neighborhood, or agency.

- A comprehensive review of treatment intervention effects and the progress made by the services provided is typically conducted at time of **termination**.

- **Clinical Social Workers** are professionals who specialize in the provision of clinical interventions to a client or client group. Generally, because of certification or licensure, a Clinical Social Worker is able to provide direct clinical services either under or with supervision, depending on legislative requirements.

- A **closed system** is a contained social system with the purpose of resisting change.

- **Closed system** is a term often used in Systems Theory and in practice with social work clients.

- A **co-dependent** is an individual who is seeking services due to problems arising from his/her relationship with an alcohol or drug users, who has formally received service for alcohol or drug abuse, and who and has a client record.

- **Cocaine**, an illicit drug derived from the leaves of the coca plant, produces feelings of euphoria, energy, alertness, confi-

dence, and heightened sensitivity. The street name for cocaine is "coke" or "snow." Generally, this drug is taken through the nostrils ("snorting"), injected with other drugs such as heroin ("speed balling"), or smoked ("freebasing").

■ A *code of ethics* is a set of statements defining the values, principles, and regulations of a profession, and regulating the conduct of its members.

■ *Codeine*, a pain-relieving drug found in some medications, is addictive when frequently used.

■ **Clinical intervention using cognitive theory concepts** focuses on the conscious thinking processes and motivations for certain behaviors. Current forms of cognitive therapy include rational-emotive therapy, reality therapy, existential therapy, and rational casework.

■ **Cognitive development** is the process by which individuals acquire the intellectual and social capacity to perceive, evaluate, and understand information.

■ Jean Piaget developed the most comprehensive **cognitive theory** by dividing human development into four stages: the sensorimotor stage, (birth to age 2), the preoperational stage (ages 2 to 7), the concrete operations stage (ages 7 to 11), and the formal operations stage (age 11 to adulthood).

■ **Collaboration** is a process in which professionals work together to provide treatment or services to a client or client group.

■ **Community self-help** refers to volunteers who provide services to others, usually with the support from an agency or community.

■ **Community organization** is an activity which involves specialized interventions used by Social Workers to assist clients or client groups with common interests or problems through planned collective action. Community organization activities may include problem identification, determining cause for the problem, developing treatment/services plans, developing strategies, acquiring and mobilizing necessary resources,

and identifying and recruiting community leaders for improving anticipated outcomes.

- **Competence** in a social services profession includes possession of all relevant educational and experiential requirements, demonstrated ability through passing licensing and certification examinations, and the ability to carry out work assignments and provide social work services while adhering to social work values.

- **Planning activities** are performed by policy-makers to coordinate information, influence/power, and resources on a broad scale in order to achieve goals. Planning activities include searching for underlying causes rather than the symptoms of human problems.

- **Comprehensive planning** seeks to facilitate the reaching of human potential rather simply to eliminate problems.

- **Social work planning** includes specifying future objectives, evaluating the means for achieving them, and making deliberate choices about appropriate courses of action.

- **Confidentiality** is an ethical principle whereby Social Workers or other professionals may not disclose information about a client without the client's consent.

- **Conflict management** is a strategy by which individuals are assisted to define the nature of their relationships, remove communication barriers, identify problems and resources, and work together to solve specific problems, generally along some time lines.

- **Conflict resolution** is the elimination of problems arising when different parties or groups compete for the same resources or goals. This activity occurs by facilitating compromises, achieving accommodation, or sometimes by the surrender of one group to the other. Social Workers engage in conflict resolution when they clarify, educate, mediate, and recommend alternative options to a client or client group.

- **Consultation** is a professional relationship between an individual in need of special expertise to solve a specific problem and an agency which possesses it.

- A **contract** is a written, oral, or implied agreement between a client or client group and the Social Worker, outlining the goals, methods, timetables, and mutual obligations to be fulfilled during the treatment/service process.

- **Contracting** is a process in which goals, methods, and mutual obligations of treatment/services are discussed, leading to a formal agreement regarding services.

- A **control group** is a set of subjects who are matched in every possible respect with another group but who are not provided or exposed to the intervention or variable being studied.

- **Controlled substances** are drugs that are strictly regulated or outlawed, such as marijuana, narcotics, stimulants, depressants, and hallucinogens.

- **Correlation coefficient** is a numerical index of the extent to which two variables are related.

- **Correlation** is a statistical method used to determine relationship between variables and pattern of variation between two situations where change in one is associated with change in the other.

- **Cost-benefit analysis** is an administration and management activity in which organizational goals are evaluated along with the expenses and resources required to achieve them.

- *Cotherapy* includes services or intervention provided on behalf of a client or client group whereby two or more professionals work in collaboration in the delivery of the interventions.

- **Crisis theory** is a set of concepts concerning people's reactions when confronted with new or unfamiliar experiences, such as natural disasters, significant loss, changes in social status, or life-cycle changes.

- **Crisis interventions** include activities that provide information about the availability of services and/or provide services directly to a person on an outpatient basis when the individual is in need of immediate attention. Crisis interventions are a clinical practice employed to assist clients or client groups engage in change which is directed towards positive coping, growth, and learning new behaviors for coping with similar experiences or situations.

- A **crisis** is either an internal or social experience of distress in which an event disrupts some essential functions of existing social institutions. The outcome of a crisis can be positive if the individual eventually finds new coping mechanisms to deal with the unfamiliar event, thus adding to his repertoire of effective adaptive responses.

- **Cross-sectional research** is a research design in which a researcher collects data on the subject under investigation at one point in time, as in a one-time survey; it may also be a comparison of subjects who represent different aspects of a single variable.

- **Cross-tabulation** is a method for assessing the relationship between two variables using tabular methods.

- **Cultural relativism**, both a philosophy and a perspective for understanding, suggests that specific norms or rituals can only be understood accurately in the context of a culture's goals, social history, and environmental demands.

- **Cultural deprivation** refers to the absence of certain socialization experiences that an individual may need in order to cope effectively in social situations that are different from past experiences. An individual or group of individuals deprived of specific cultural experiences may often lack social skills, values, or attitudes needed to effectively deal with differing cultures.

- **Cultural lag** refers to the retention of customs, habits, and technologies even though they have become obsolete or irrelevant to new standards set by the prevailing culture.

- The customs, habits, skills, knowledge, technology, arts, science, religious and political behaviors of a group of people are its *culture*.

- *Decertification* is a process whereby an individual's professional titles, certification or licensure, and privileges are removed because of non-compliance with or violation of predetermined qualifications, criteria, or standards.

- *Detoxification services*, typically provided in hospital in-patient, non-hospital residential or ambulatory care settings, provide immediate and short term medical services specific for dealing with withdrawal from substance dependency.

- *Detoxification* is a treatment service directed towards the medically supervised elimination of the physical and/or psychological dependence on a substance/chemical.

- *Discharge planning* helps clients better manage their concerns after direct services are discontinued.

- *Termination* is the phase of treatment or services when a client's involvement with a treatment program is concluded and the program no longer bears responsibility for the client's care.

- *Drug dependence* is the abuse and dependence on substances, resulting in drug addiction.

- *Eligibility* is the meeting of specific qualifications required to obtain or be granted specific benefits.

- *Empirically based practice* is social work practice in which a worker uses research as a problem-solving tool for the evaluation of practice effectiveness.

- In social work practice, the *enabler role* refers to those activities which assist the client or client group in becoming able to deal with stress by use of empathy, dealing with emotions and thoughts, and the identification of client strengths.

- *Encounter group* is a form of group treatment or intervention, usually intense and short-term, whose major purpose is to promote personal growth through communication and discussions.

- An *episode* is a continuous period of care which may involve multiple services.

- *Social work ethics* are moral principles resulting in conduct that is practiced by social work professionals.

- *Ethnic-sensitive practice* is social work practice that values the capabilities, distinctive cultural histories, and needs of people of various ethnic origins.

- An *experiment* is a systematic study to test, assess, and evaluate a social or physical phenomena.

- *Facilitation* is a structured activity directed toward creating change by collecting individuals in such a manner that communication and motivations are geared toward change.

- *Family therapy* is a form of treatment in which the interventions are directed to family members as a single unit.

- In social work practice, a *family* is collection of individuals who are related by blood, adoption, or marriage and who share residences, have mutual rights, and socialize children.

- *Feasibility studies* are objective assessments of the resources needed to accomplish specified objectives.

- *Feedback*, the provision of information on results of an action to the individual who performed the action, permits a more objective evaluation of the action's effectiveness or ineffectiveness and allows for modifications in the ongoing action to increase likelihood of success. In social work administration, feedback, often used in supervision, personal evaluations, and client reports, provides objective outcome measures to achieve desired improvements and provides staff with positive indicators when they are doing good work.

- *Funding* of social work programs is the allocation of a specific amount of money to be used in carrying out an organization's program for a certain amount of time.

- *Goal-setting* is an activity performed by Social Workers to help clients clarify and define the objective they hope to achieve and to establish steps needed to complete their goals.

- **Grantsmanship**, the use of protocols for acquiring funding for a project, requires knowledge in research design, verbal communication, salesmanship, writing, assessing needs, techniques for problem solving, and political and administrative intervention, as well as knowledge of appropriate sources funding projects.

- **Group** is defined by Social Workers as a collection of individuals, brought together by mutual interest.

- **Major types of groups** include the primary group, political groups, educational groups, task groups, reference groups, and treatment groups.

- **Group treatment** provides services for emotional or cognitive disorders to several individuals in a single setting.

- **Hallucinogens** include LSD, DMT, STP, mescaline, psilocybin and peyote.

- An individual who by circumstances does not have a fixed address or shelter can be considered **homeless**.

- In social work research, a **hypothesis** is a statement or premise regarding a relationship among variables which can be observed and measured.

- **Implied consent** is an agreement to participate expressed by gestures, signs, actions, or statements that are interpreted as agreement, or by unresisting silence or inaction.

- **Infectious diseases**, such as hepatitis, venereal disease, or tuberculosis, are transmitted from one individual to another.

- **Informed consent** is the granting permission by a client to a Social Worker to use specific interventions and models in the provision of services, along with the acknowledgment of risk factors in the use of the interventions or models.

- **Inhalants** are chemicals (ether, glue, chloroform, nitrous oxide, gasoline, paint thinner, etc.) which induce an alternate state of consciousness.

- *Initial assessments* are employed during the early phase of treatment. Assessment tools tend to focus on sociological areas and take a macro view of the issues, interventions, and treatment models.

- *Initial clinical assessments* assist in the development of the most appropriate treatment model.

- *Clinical assessment* can include psychological testing, summary of psychosocial assessments, and developmental testing.

- *Intake* refers to the initial treatment/services activities used by social agencies, including informing the client about the services provided and conditions of services. Intake is performed for the purpose of obtaining information and impressions of the nature of the problem and assigning the client to the social work provider.

- *Intervention*, in social work, usually involves talk with the purpose of improving the emotional and cognitive condition of the clients. Interventions are the end result of clinical models, approaches, strategies, and paradigms.

- *Social work interviews* are purposeful interactions among individuals with the intent to improve, clarify, or understand a specific problem. Social work interviews may be conducted with individuals, groups, families, and communities and may be directive, nondirective, or fact-gathering.

- The accumulated information, data and, scientific findings of a particular profession is its **knowledge base**.

- *Licensure* is a governmental function that grants organizations the right to carry out a regulated activity.

- *Long-term programs* are designed to provide extended services to clients with chronic problems who are ambulatory and who require a controlled environment and supportive therapy for an indefinite period of time, but who are not in need of nursing, medical, or psychiatric care.

- In social work, **macro practice** refers to activities directed toward improving or changing the social order, including such

efforts as political action, community organization, education, and advocacy. Social Workers interested in macro practice take into account the sociopolitical, historical, economic, and environmental forces which affect the human condition.

■ **Malpractice** is behavior by a professional that violates the code of ethics and proves harmful to the client. Malpractice may result in termination of certification or licensure.

■ **Management tasks** are fundamental activities performed by managers to meet the goals of the organization or agency. Management tasks include creating and evaluating programs; securing financial resources; designing organizational structures, staff functions, and roles; and evaluating overall organizational ability to provide needed services.

■ The **medical model of assistance** to individuals tends to focus on the illness to be treated, with less attention to the client's social, emotional, or cognitive concerns.

■ A **mental status examination** is an evaluation to determine a client's level of psychosocial, intellectual, and emotional functioning and orientation as to time, person, and place.

■ **Methadone** treatment includes methadone maintenance or detoxification. **Methadone** is used as an oral substitute for opiates during the rehabilitative phase of treatment. It is also used with those clients who are being withdrawn (detoxified) from maintenance treatment.

■ **Methadone maintenance** is the continued administration of methadone, at relatively stable dosage levels, in conjunction with social and medical services.

■ In social work, **micro practice** activities focus on the client's psychosocial conflicts. Micro practice is designed to assist in solving problems experienced by individuals, families, and small groups.

■ A **mission** is a series of statements identifying efforts or activities critical in the effective accomplishment of predetermined abstract or concrete ideals by an individual, agency, or profession.

- A *monitoring report* in social work is a detailed document clearly outlining in sequence all activities engaged in by a Social Worker. A monitoring report is a summary of efforts and technical assistance provided, mandated, and suggested, designed to assess a program's ability to deliver services, its special needs, and its development over time.

- In social work, *negotiation* is a structured activity for the gathering of individuals who are in opposition or competing for a scarce resources and assisting them through the use of fair communications, bargaining, and compromise.

- An *objective interview* is a structured interview in which the Social Worker attempts to acquire specific information from the client by asking specific questions. Objective interviews, which tend not be therapeutic, are generally conducted during the intake phase of treatment/services.

- *Outcomes* are situations, circumstances, or conditions that occur as a consequence of the implementation or manipulation of variables.

- *Outcome evaluation* is a research process aimed at determining whether a program is achieving its objectives and whether the results are due to the predetermined interventions.

- *Outpatient services* are services provided to a client lasting two or more hours per day for three or more days per week.

- *Regulatory licensure* occurs at the Associate, Baccalaureate, Intermediate, Advanced, and Clinical levels.

- *Certification* is offered by Board Certified Diplomat, Academy of Certified Social Workers and Diplomat.

- Areas of *specialization* in social work are Practice, Research, Clinical, and Community.

- The *fields of knowledge* in Social Work are finite.

- The *first credentialing legislation* was passed in 1934 (Puerto Rico) and in 1945 (California). In the 1960s further legislation was passed regarding social work licensure, and during

the 1970s thirteen states passed credentialing legislation for the first time.

- **Licensing examinations** are designed to test entry-level skills and abilities.

- **Knowledge, skills, and abilities** are tasks needed to perform those activities delegated to Social Workers upon entry into the work force.

- When taking a **multiple choice examination**, eliminating wrong answers may help you to arrive at the correct one.

- **Take your time** when answering a question. Never pounce on an answer, for most questions offer you the correct answer plus several really attractive choices.

- When reading a question, always ask yourself, **"What are they testing here?"**

- **Key words** such as **first, best, most** tell you that the item writer wants you to discard certain answers because they wouldn't be done first or that there may be two possible answers, one slightly better than the other.

- Before you look at the four possible answers, **think of the answer in your own words**. See if that answer resonates with any of the listed answers.

- Always factor in the **social work bias**. Social Workers, particularly those who teach and those who examine, tend to be liberal in their world view.

- If you haven't a clue about an answer to a question, mark the question to return to it and **answer all those you know first**.

- There is no right answer to any question; there is just the answer that the examination committee and the testing service are looking for.

- Focusing on what answer the testers are looking for, rather than what is the **correct** answer, will help you succeed.

- Keep things simple: do not go beyond the information given to you by the stem or the answers. **Think like a Social Worker,**

and remember that you have completed a program from a school of social work.

- The national social work examination is in transition.

- If you take the examination on computer, become familiar with one before you go for the test.

- Don't go beyond what is written in the stem of a question, and don't add anything when you read the question.

- Social Workers train to be clinicians, administrators, educators, researchers, community organizers, and politicians.

- The profession of social work allows for the integration of various disciplines such as psychology, economics, anthropology and sociology in the generation of models, approaches, and interventions used by professional Social Workers.

- *Human socialization* is best defined as "becoming a human being." Human beings become who they are because of their genetic makeup and social pressures. Human beings are influenced by major social factors: family, religion, community, education, government, and self.

- *Family values* have had a great influence on what you think and feel and how you behave.

- *Family* is the primary source of one's understanding of the world, one's self, and others.

- *Religion* influences our understanding of spirituality, world events, and their relationship.

- *Community*, made up of the friends and neighbors where we live, influences the creation of one's world.

- *Education and school* play a role in making you the person you have become with the perceptions you have created.

- *Government and political situations and events* have also molded who you have become.

- For Social Workers, understanding the factors which contributed to the molding of the individual is important information in assessment.

- **Alcoholism** is a leader in automobile deaths, family problems, depression, and medical and employment problems.

- Approximately 11 million Americans suffer from alcoholism or alcohol dependence and approximately 7 million from alcohol abuse.

- Alcoholism is physical or psychological dependence on alcohol use, leading to social, mental, financial, interpersonal, and physical impairment.

- In **primary alcoholism**, the individual has a high tolerance for alcohol, drinks in response to physiological withdrawal symptoms, and puts drinking ahead of all other activities.

- **Secondary alcoholism** includes such concerns as those of individuals who are experiencing a major psychiatric disorder before the onset of drinking problems. The most common symptom of secondary alcoholism is affective disorder and antisocial personality disorder.

- **Reactive alcoholism** is characterized by heavy or excessive drinking that starts soon after experiencing a perceived crisis, such as the death of a loved one, surviving an accident, or crime victimization.

- The two most often used **classification systems of alcohol abuse and dependence** are the Diagnostic and Statistical Manual of Mental Disorders (DSM-IV) and the International Classification of Diseases (ICD).

- **Tolerance** is the need for markedly increased amounts of alcohol to achieve intoxication or desired effect, or markedly diminished effect with continued use of the same amount of alcohol.

- **Withdrawal** refers to symptoms experienced when no alcohol is consumed, or a need to take alcohol or closely related substance to relieve or avoid such symptoms.

- A **diagnosis of alcohol abuse** requires that one or more of the following four criteria occur at any time during the same 12-month period: recurrent alcohol use resulting in a failure to

fulfill major role obligations at work, school, or home; recurrent alcohol use in situations in which it is physically hazardous; recurrent alcohol-related legal problems; and continued alcohol use despite persistent or recurrent social or interpersonal problems caused or exacerbated by the effects of alcohol.

- For the Social Worker to arrive at a diagnosis of alcohol abuse, the client must never have met the criteria for alcohol dependence.

- Long-term use of substantial amounts of alcohol can result in diarrhea, gastritis, pancreatitis, fatty liver, alcoholic hepatitis, and cirrhosis.

- Heavy drinking is also related to increased risk of cancer of the mouth, tongue, pharynx, esophagus, stomach, colon, liver, and pancreas.

- Alcoholics often develop degenerative heart disease, nutritional deficiencies, and acute and chronic brain damage.

- Alcoholic women often suffer from infertility and a high frequency of gynecologic problems.

- Alcohol abuse during pregnancy can result in harm to the fetus ranging from mild physical and behavioral deficits to fetal alcohol syndrome.

- Between 6 million and 12 million children live in households with at least one alcoholic parent.

- Although a large proportion of these children in alcoholic households function well and do not develop serious problems, they are at risk for alcoholism and a variety of cognitive, emotional, and behavioral difficulties.

- Children from alcoholic families tend to have lower I.Q., verbal, and reading scores, but still perform within normal ranges.

- Children from alcoholic families report higher levels of depression and anxiety than children from nonalcoholic families, and are frequently diagnosed as having conduct disorders.

- Despite numerous studies that show an association between alcoholism and violence in the family, causality remains in doubt.

- When compared to nonalcoholic families, families of alcoholics have lower levels of family cohesion, expressiveness, independence, and intellectual orientation and higher levels of conflict.

- During the past few years social work has generated a tremendous amount of literature in the area of substance abuse treatment.

- The *enabler* is generally defined as a significant other who, because of his own needs, encourages, promotes, or supports the continued consumption of alcohol, addiction, and abuse.

- The social work examination is based not on social work curricula, but rather on the tasks that Social Workers perform.

- Social Workers who work with alcoholics make good use of Alcoholics Anonymous as a resource.

- *Protection of children* from parents is a recent social concern.

- *Children* throughout history have been held low in the social and political order; they were understood more as possessions or important contributors to the work force than as persons in need of care, affection, and attention.

- *Child abuse and neglect* is best defined as the physical or mental injury, sexual abuse or exploitation, negligence, or maltreatment of a child by an individual responsible for that child.

- Dealing with child abuse and neglect includes distinguishing poverty from neglect, keeping the family together whenever possible, and avoiding protective intervention solely for reasons of the parents' moral standing.

- Female children were more likely to be sexually abused than males; however, this finding may reflect that sexual abuse involving females was more likely to be reported.

- Fatalities as a result of abuse were more frequent among younger children, and moderate injuries more prevalent among older children.

- Although the number of abuse and neglect cases reported to child protective services has increased by 57 percent since 1980, only 44 percent of the cases known to professionals were investigated by child protective services.

- Of the children known to be abused or neglected 56 percent were not investigated or served by child protective services.

- It is difficult to determine the etiology of abuse and neglect because so many factors directly contribute to sexual abuse, physical abuse, and neglect.

- Research suggests that no single factor can explain the occurrence of child abuse and neglect.

- Reports of neglect far outnumber reports of physical abuse.

- Poverty is repeatedly identified as a major factor in abuse and neglect.

- Providing services in the area of child abuse and neglect is fundamental to the profession of social work.

- Social Workers have taken pride in the identification, assessment, and treatment of child abuse and neglect.

- Traditionally, child protection agencies hired professionally trained Social Workers who relied heavily on the casework model to ameliorate family ills and thereby protect children at risk.

- Since the mid-1970s, there has been much less attention to casework and more emphasis on providing hard services, goal-directed intervention, and case management.

- Generally, most of the services provided in this area require Social Workers to possess assessment skills, contracting skills, and a significant knowledge of state protection agencies.

- *Assessment skills* require a fundamental ability to consider and organize critical information about the circumstances lead-

ing to abuse and neglect and require the use of clinical contract to include the child, the Social Worker, and significant others in the recovery process.

- In many cases the child protection agency's responsibility includes responding to the dramatic increase in the number of reports of child abuse and neglect.

- In 1993 there were just under 3 million reports of child abuse or neglect, with a substantiation rate of approximately 34 percent.

- Family and juvenile courts, working with child protection service agencies, will, as appropriate, declare children in need of protection, remove children from their parents' custody and place them in the custody of child protective service agencies, and approve children's placement in out-of-home care. The major responsibility of the Social Worker is to ensure the immediate safety of the child.

- **Drug abuse**, like alcoholism is a major social problem in American society.

- Drug abuse cuts across cultural, social, economic, political, and educational boundaries and results in the destruction of the American social fabric.

- Drug abuse is the inappropriate use of a substance in a manner destructive to one's emotional, physical, social, and cognitive abilities.

- Drug abuse is addictive, resulting in a physiological and psychological dependence.

- A number of methods exist for the placement of substances into the brain. The most effective method is to inhale the substance; injected or swallowed substances reach the brain less quickly.

- In general, there are **four major classifications of drugs** that tend to be abused: stimulants, hallucinogens, depressants/sedatives/hypnotics and narcotics/analgesics/opioids.

- **Stimulants** consist of amphetamines/methamphetamine and cocaine.

- **Physical effects of amphetamines/ methamphetamine** include increased heart rate and elevated blood pressures. When taken in large dosages, amphetamines/methamphetamine will increase oxygen consumption and body temperature.

- **Psychological effects of amphetamines/methamphetamine** consist of an increased sense of well-being, energy, dizziness, insomnia, and euphoria. High dosages of amphetamines/methamphetamine may cause psychosis, paranoia, and delusions.

- **Physical effects of cocaine** include rapid heart rates and blood pressure, and some pupillary dilation. High dosages may cause depressed respiration, heart failure, and seizures.

- **Hallucinogens** include cannabinoids, LSD (lysergic acid diethylamide), mescaline, phencyclidine, and psilocybin.

- The **physical effects of cannabinoids** include increased heart rate and pulse, reduced vision, increased appetite, and decreased coordination.

- **Psychological effects of cannabinoids** consist of euphoria, reduction of inhibitions, apathy, hallucinations, and perceptual distortion of both space and time.

- **Physical effects of LSD** include dilated pupils, elevated blood sugar and body temperature, loss of coordination, and increased salivation and tearing.

- **Psychological effects of LSD** may include visual illusions, alterations in sound and colors, changes in mood, and extreme anxiety. LSD abuse can result in a sense of euphoria and depersonalization.

- **Physical effects of mescaline** include increased perspiration, tremors, increased blood pressure and heart rate, a decreased appetite, and vomiting.

- **Psychological effects of mescaline** include hallucinations, extreme anxiety, and distortion of senses.

- *Phencyclidine's physical effects* include increased blood pressure, sweating, vomiting, and seizures.

- *Psychological effects of phencyclidine* include the experience of a psychotic state, euphoria, and an appearance of intoxication.

- *Psilocybin's physical effects* include elevated blood pressure, respiratory rates, and body temperature, as well as some pupillary dilation and abdominal cramps.

- *Depressants/sedatives/hypnotics* include barbiturates, benzodiazepines, and methaqualone.

- *Physical effects of barbiturates* include decreased heart rates, blood pressure, and respiration.

- *Psychological effects of depressants/sedatives/hypnotics* include sedation, euphoria, decreased mental acuity, and slowed speech.

- *Physical effects of benzodiazepines* include depression, dizziness, nausea, and dry mouth.

- *Methaqualone's physical effects* are increased motor activity, dry mouth, loss of appetite, and vomiting.

- *Psychological effects of methaqualone* are feelings of euphoria, sedation, increased self-confidence, and increased sexual arousal.

- *Narcotics/analgesics/opioids* consist of methadone, opiates, and propoxyphene.

- *Methadone's physical effects* include decreased response to pain, dizziness, sedation, pupillary constriction, blurred vision, increased perspiration, and reduced respiratory rate.

- *Psychological effects of methadone* include euphoria and reduction in mental function.

- *Opiates' physical effects* are a decrease in sensation of and emotional response to pain, dizziness, sedation, pupillary construction, vomiting, and reduced respiratory rate.

- *Propoxyphene's physical effects* include pupillary constriction, blurred vision, headaches, and vomiting.

- *Propoxyphene's psychological effects* include euphoria, mild depression, confusion, and delusions or hallucinations.

- Understanding child sexual abuse includes studying such issues as the incest taboo, characteristics of sexual offenders and child victims, and recognition and identification of child victims.

- The definition of **child sexual abuse** encompasses a broad range of non-consensual sexual behaviors involving children and includes sexual acts accomplished by force and activities committed by an adult or a significantly older child or adolescent with a child.

- Sexual abuse of children includes penetration, sexual touching, voyeurism, and sexual exposure. The defining characteristic of sexual abuse is that the child does not or cannot give consent because of coercion or significant inequality in age, size, knowledge, or position in the relationship.

- Sexual abuse of children is accomplished in a variety of ways. Force, threat of force, or the fear of injury or death occurs in a substantial percentage of cases

- An **operational definition of child sexual abuse** includes forced, tricked, or manipulated contact with a child by an older person with the purpose of the sexual gratification of the older person.

- In some cases of sexual abuse of children, a young child may be forced to play games involving pretending to be like an adult.

- For many types of sexual abuse of children, it is difficult to determine whether the behavior has the intent of sexual gratification. The critical point for Social Workers is that many behaviors should alert the professional to the fact that the child (or family) may need services.

- Characteristics of childhood sexual abuse range from fondling to intercourse.

- Several investigators have documented that more serious sexual acts tend to occur in intra-family abuse cases rather than in extra-family cases.

- Children of virtually all age groups have been identified following victimization, although as might be expected, abuse of young children and infants is difficult to document.

- Girls are more likely to be identified for abuse, although current trends seem to indicate that abuse of boys is an underreported but growing problem.

- Currently, clinical samples consist of about 20 percent male victims. About 70 percent of victims are abused more than once, and many victims are abused over significant portions of their childhood.

- Sexual abuse of children is a significant and relatively common problem of childhood.

- It is associated with a wide range of psychosocial problems in childhood and adulthood and may be an underlying reason why clients seek social work services.

- The failure to screen for childhood sexual abuse (and family violence in general) may be regarded in the near future as a form of social work malpractice.

- An interesting assessment principle learned in the past decade or so is that one of the best ways to identify victims is to ask clients about their experiences. Although not every victimized person will tell the first professional who asks, and many victims (very young children, for example) present special assessment problems for the Social Worker, many people will report histories of childhood sexual abuse if asked.

- There has been little research regarding the various ways that children disclose abuse.

- Children disclose abuse in subtle ways, through behavioral changes reflecting anxiety or stress (nightmares or fearfulness,

for example), through sexual behaviors or statements, or through disguised statements to peers or adults.

- Some children disclose abuse only when asked about it, whereas others disclose abuse in clear, precise statements after the first incidence.

- Children tend to lack the intellectual or verbal abilities to describe what did or did not happen to them.

- Children's inability to verbalize concerns, along with fear and anxiety, makes their treatment difficult.

- Sexually abused children have been shown to have significantly lower self-esteem than other children, to be more depressed, and to exhibit sexual behavior problems more often.

- *Long-term effects of childhood abuse* include posttraumatic behaviors, cognitive distortions, altered emotionality (depression and anxiety), dissociation, impaired self-reference, disturbed relatedness, avoidance, and the abuse of substances.

- Ethnicity is not necessarily associated with differences in rates of sexual abuse, but it is associated with differences in abusive experiences, offender-victim relationships, and family characteristics.

- The *"child sexual abuse accommodation syndrome"* identifies the psychological dynamics of sexual abuse situations that may account for this behavior. Sexual abuse is most often aversive or frightening, and unpleasant emotions may be evoked when the experiences are recalled.

- Since 1960, the *suicide rate* among youths ages 15 to 19 has increased from 3.6 to 11.3 per 100,000.

- *Suicide*, accounting for 14 percent of all deaths in this age group, is the third leading cause of death among youths, trailing only accidents and homicide.

- Depressed youths are at higher risk of suicide, and drug abuse has been found to be particularly high among suicide attempters and completers.

- Substance abuse has also been identified as one element of a syndrome of delinquent behaviors. Poverty has been linked to higher school-leaving and youth unemployment rates.

- Suicide among adolescents, as with adults, is most highly correlated with an active psychiatric episode, specifically depressive or bipolar disorders. Estimates suggest that 90 percent of all adolescent suicides occur in psychiatrically disordered individuals.

- Substance abuse and conduct disorder are also associated with suicide by youths.

- A *predictor of future suicide*, especially for young men: 40 percent of youth attempters will make future attempts, and 10 percent to 40 percent of adolescent attempters eventually die by suicide.

- More than one-third of adolescents who successfully commit suicide are intoxicated at the time of death, and many more may be using other drugs; those who commit suicide via firearms are more likely to be using substances.

- Of the 10 percent of adolescent suicides not associated with psychiatric illness, the most distinguishing variable may be access to a loaded gun.

- Over the years the study of *mental retardation* has involved Social Workers in the development of more sensitive and comprehensive treatment plans for children.

- The fundamental knowledge required in the assessment and diagnosis of mental retardation has been clearly laid out by both the professions of psychology and psychiatry.

- The major factors in the assessment and diagnosis of mental retardation include significant limitations in adaptive functioning in at least two of the following skill areas: communication, self-care, home living, social/interpersonal skills, use of community resources, self-direction, functional academic skills, work, leisure, health, and safety.

- A second factor in the assessment and diagnosis of mental retardation is the level of severity, reflecting the level of intellectual impairment.

- The *four levels of severity*, reflecting levels of intellectual impairment, are Mild, Moderate, Severe, and Profound. The best source for a comprehensive description of the severity of mental retardation is the DSM-IV.

- Persons with **mild retardation** are generally referred to as "educable." They can achieve social and vocational skills for adequate social functioning.

- Persons with **moderate retardation** are generally referred to as "trainable," They can achieve social and vocational skill for adequate social functioning but are not likely to progress beyond the second grade. As adults they may engage in unskilled or semiskilled employment with supervision.

- Persons with **severe retardation** generally do not possess communication skills or speech during early childhood. Severely retarded persons may be trained to talk and to perform simple self-care tasks.

- **Profound retardation** involves dysfunction in the area of sensorimotor function. Profoundly retarded persons need a constant care giver and close supervision in a controlled setting.

- When dealing with the issue of **disability**, one difficulty is agreeing on a definition of disability.

- The Americans with Disabilities Act of 1990 stated that 43 million people have issues regarding disabilities, whereas other estimates say the number is at least 14.5 % of the population

- People with low levels of education and income have higher instances of disabilities.

- Since the 1960s people with disabilities and those who support them have worked to change the general perception that people with disabilities are helpless and unable to cope with life in general.

- They also make the point that people with disabilities suffer as much as or more from discrimination than they do with their disability.

- **Psychodynamic Paradigm**: Created by Sigmund Freud and embellished by his students, this paradigm emphasizes the importance of unconscious forces in mental life, conflict between biological instincts and society's demands, and early childhood experiences.

- **Humanistic Paradigms**: Ideas which emphasize that a person's capacity for personal growth, freedom to chose one's destiny, and self-understanding are critical for understanding behavior, and that behavior change can occur through the use of a nurturing and warm professional relationship.

- **Social Learning Paradigm**: A set of ideas which emphasize the scientific study of behavior and its environmental determinants. This paradigm argues that individuals engage in specific behaviors because of environmental conditions experienced as rewards.

- **Social Systems Paradigm**: A set of ideas which emphasize that behavior is influenced by social/physical environmental factors such as community, family, neighborhood, peer group, and school. The paradigm also argues that behavioral changes can occur as a result of applying interventions to specific parts of the client's social, emotional, and cognitive system.

- In the process of acquiring a comprehensive understanding of Clinical Social Work, it is very important to keep treatment processes and structures in mind, especially when working toward change with a particular client.

- The treatment structure created or adopted by the Clinical Social Worker is a road map or perspective for the models and interventions that the Clinical Social Worker will use in treatment.

- **Paradigm**: A set of ideas which account for behavior. Human behavior is explained by employing concepts embraced by the supported paradigm's ideas.

- **Model**: A definite set of approaches, founded on or supported by a paradigm, which offers a distinct means for attacking a psychological concern.

- **Approach**: A pre-planned means for dealing with a particular set of psychological concerns within the boundaries of the paradigm.

- **Strategy**: A planned process for delivery of specific interventions with an anticipated outcome of intervention effects.

- **Intervention**: A set of pre-planned works or physical movements designed to elicit an emotional, cognitive, or psychical response from an individual in hope of producing self-awareness and self-improvement.

- **Psychodynamic theory** provides a taxonomy for behavioral change, allows for character, typically requires insight, is long term, has helped in the establishment of foundations for modern psychology.

- In psychodynamic theory, human behavior is considered to be an outcome of unconscious impulses.

- **Social learning theory** is very amenable to research, establishes clear behavioral outcomes, and encourages the use of baseline data.

- **Humanistic theory**, based on a psychotherapeutic approach, uses the interpersonal relationship as a tool for creating change and supports the ideas that social factors influence behavior and that behavioral change is a result of social interaction.

- **Social system theory**, a comprehensive theory for intervention, is not well researched, supports the idea that change is possible at multiple levels, is used by a variety of professions to understand human behavior, encourages the analysis of social change, and establishes human behavior as an outcome

- The major purpose of the **client record** is the documentation of client progress based on services provided, collection of relevant information regarding the client's history and clinical

needs, and demonstration of the process involved in management of the services provided to the client.

- In most social work settings, the clinical record is based on the model which supports a series of services such as assessment, treatment planning, termination, and aftercare.

- The clinical record is used as a tool for improvement or assessment of clinical practice.

- The clinical record provides the Social Worker with a method for documentation and a means for assessment of a client's progress.

- The main purpose for documentation of clinical activities is to ensure that all interventions provided to the client and progress made by the client are recorded in a consistent, timely, and professional manner.

- A fundamental truism in clinical social work practice: "If it is not in the clinical record, it did not happen."

- It is critical for the Clinical Social Worker to develop a structured method for the collection and documentation of clinical data which, in time, will provide information regarding the services needed by and provided to the client.

- The *treatment phases* are referral, intake, assessment, diagnosis, treatment plan development and execution, treatment plan review and execution, clinical progress recording, termination, and aftercare.

- *Initial collection of data* establishes a clinically based foundation for the eventual assessment of the client's concern, selection of a diagnosis, and employment of a specialized treatment plan.

- *Basic referral and intake data* assists in the establishment of clinical scope, parameters, and focus necessary for the eventual implementation of appropriate, effective, and relevant clinical interventions.

- The *referral phase* includes the collection of initial client data regarding a the client's concern.

- Referral data assists in the initial assessment of the client's concern, identification of resources required to deal with the concern, and potential organization of resources and professionals to deal with the concern.

- Referral data assists in the matching of agency/professional services with the client's concerns, location of the services, and a time for initiating services.

- **Intake** is that aspect of the treatment process in which demographic and basic fundamental clinical information is acquired for the potential matching of the client with the Social Worker.

- In the intake phase of treatment, the Social Worker and the client begin the process of specifically defining the clinical needs of the client and assessing the potential therapeutic models to be utilized and interventions to be employed.

- The intake phase allows the Social Worker to establish the clinical program to be implemented in dealing with the client's concerns, time required for dealing with the concerns, and an initial assessment of the potential treatment or services required.

- An important aspect of the intake process is the acquisition of basic data which may be used during the assessment phase.

- Data such as the client's current health status, age, economic and employment status, racial/ethnic background, religious background, parents' child rearing style, and educational level may also be collected during the intake phase.

- Assessment of the client's history, present clinical condition, and needed services is basic in the provision of treatment services.

- The major purpose for the **assessment phase** is the collection and integration of clinical information leading to the selection of a diagnosis and the development of a treatment plan, specific to the client, which will result in the provision of the most effective interventions possible.

- The assessment phase includes the collection of clinical data through the use of the clinical interview, client self report, psychological instruments, psychosocial assessment, and case consultations.

- Clinical assessment phase includes problem identification, treatment plan development, and selection of treatment approach.

- Clinical assessment includes collection of data which assists in understanding the client's psychosocial development, interpersonal relationships with family and significant others, interpersonal skills development, consistent and chronological age, role in the family, mental status, and cognitive ability.

- An important aspect of the assessment phase is developing an understanding of the various factors which have contributed to the client's concern.

- The **treatment plan phase** involves activities which result in the selection, implementation, evaluation, and recording of interventions specifically designed to resolve the client's concerns.

- The treatment plan generally articulates the client's clinical concerns, precipitating factors leading to the need for services, the clinical contract, the clinical goals (long-term/short-term), and a statement which may include a description of either the model or theory to be employed when dealing with the concern.

- The initial activity performed during the treatment planning phase is the in-depth review of referral, intake, assessment, and diagnostic data.

- A critical aspect of treatment planning is the clinical articulation of the client's concerns.

- Through the integration of the client's appraisal and the Social Worker's assessment, a more developed and refined statement of the concern may be acquired.

- The **concern (problem) statement** becomes the focus of treatment and anchors clinical efforts and selection of interventions.

- Once the client's initial and assessment data has been reviewed, the client's concern defined, and a diagnosis assigned, a clinical contract can be negotiated.

- The *clinical contract* is an implicit statement which defines the client's and the Social Worker's responsibilities for dealing with the problems.

- The clinical contract provides the direction needed for the development of clinical objectives and goals which, when met, will illustrate the progress made toward solving the client's concern.

- Clinical objectives and goals, typically guided by time lines, are the main indicators of clinical effectiveness.

- A generally forgotten aspect of clinical treatment planning is the **identification of a treatment model or approach** to be used in selecting relevant interventions.

- A fundamental clinical question regarding model or approach selection is "What treatment paradigm will be most useful to employ?"

- Clinical treatment planning involves matching of the client's concern with potential interventions, identification and employment of a treatment model or approach sensitive to the client's needs, and matching of the interventions with the client's therapeutic needs.

- The primary importance for **treatment review** is assessment of intervention effectiveness, monitoring of progress made toward meeting treatment objectives, and identification of concerns which, if resolved, may further assist the client's recovery.

- Review of treatment accomplished or required changes is important to the overall treatment process primarily because of the inherent assurance of quality.

- Treatment review provides for a periodic review of progress made toward meeting treatment plan goals.

- The treatment review phase encourages the identification of additional treatment concerns and integration of the treatment process toward dealing with these concerns.

- *Process/progress recording* is important to the treatment process because it provides the Social Worker and client a means for connecting the work achieved during treatment with the goals and objectives outlined in the treatment plan.

- The *termination phase* of treatment includes the collection of data relevant for summarizing the treatment experience and also for identification of concerns which require attention either immediately or a later time.

- During the termination phase an assessment is conducted of the treatment work and its effectiveness in solving the client's concern, and whether further treatment is required or may be of value to the client.

- The *aftercare phase* of treatment includes the assessment of the overall treatment experience(s) along with a case management plan for the continued delivery of needed services.

- The **DSM-IV** is a comprehensive categorization document developed by psychiatry for the purpose of delineating major mental health disorders.

- The DSM-IV definition of **mental disorder** is a clinically significant behavioral or psychological syndrome or pattern that is associated with present distress or with a significantly increased risk of suffering, death, pain disability, or an important loss of freedom.

- The **DSM-IV categorization of mental disorders** provides Social Workers a comprehensive method for understanding the many and varied mental health disorders.

■ There are sixteen major or global DSM-IV classifications:

1) Disorders diagnosed in infancy, childhood or adolescence

2) Delirium dementia and amnestic and other cognitive disorders

3) Mental disorders due to a general medical condition not elsewhere classified

4) Substance abuse related disorders

5) Schizophrenia and other psychotic disorders

6) Mood disorders

7) Anxiety disorders

8) Somatoform disorders

9) Factitious disorders

10) Dissociated disorders

11) Sexual and gender identity disorders

12) Eating disorders

13) Sleep disorders

14) Impulse-control disorders not elsewhere classified

15) Personality disorders

16) Other conditions that may be a focus of clinical attention.

■ DSM-IV includes a **multiaxial system** by which the Clinical Social Worker may assess several axes, each of which takes in different clinical information, and which is useful in planning treatment and anticipating a clinical outcome.

■ As a Social Worker acquires information for each axis, he or she is better able to communicate information, to understand the complexity of the clinical situation, and to encourage use of biosociopsychological model for understanding the client.

- The DSM-IV provides the Clinical Social Worker an organized way to seek out, integrate, and communicate clinical information with other mental health professionals.

- *Axis I* is dedicated to clinical disorders except for personality disorders and mental retardation.

- *Axis II* is dedicated to the reporting of personality disorders and mental retardation.

- *Axis III* is used for reporting current medical conditions that may be of relevance in either understanding or better managing the client's mental disorder.

- *Axis IV* is used for reporting psychosocial and environmental problems which may influence the overall diagnosis, treatment, and recovery of the clients.

- Axis IV is where the Social Worker is able to report clinical judgment regarding the individual's overall level of social functioning. Assessment of the client's social functioning is done by using the Global Assessment of Function (GAF) Scale.

- The *Global Assessment of Function Scale*, which assists in tracking the client's progress in treatment at different times, provides a measurement of how well the client is functioning in a social context at the present time.

- It is generally easier to work with individuals or groups of individuals who are interested, motivated, and willing to work on their concerns.

- Through the development of a *positive working clinical relationship*, an individual who is not motivated or is "resisting" treatment may become open to the possibility of treatment.

- The use of *empathy* (positive regard, non-judgmental attitude, and non-possessive warmth) may be of most value during the early part of the relationship-building process.

- *Professional relationship* is the tool from which motivation for treatment develops. It assists in reducing resistance, espe-

cially if the individual or group is not willing to engage in the treatment process.

- **Human services organizations** are typically organized around a set of social values and funding requirements.

- Human services organizations are developed and implemented to either solve or manage a concern.

- In most cases, human services activities are guided by ideals, philosophies, objectives, and goals which exist for the structuring of the staff's activities and efforts.

- Philosophical positions held by individuals or communities have a direct and significant effect on the type and quality of services/interventions to be disseminated.

- In most cases, the community's philosophical positions and vision set the stage either for creating a special social delivery system or providing resources to an existing delivery system.

- Once a social problem is identified and an investment (funding) is made by the community, it is possible to define the mission of the human services delivery system.

- The **mission** of an agency or a community activity is a clear statement which globally defines the needs or what will be accomplished.

- **Mission statements** set boundaries for the creation of policy and procedures, define rules and regulations for the organization, and help to determine what types of professionals are needed to deal with the social problem.

- Missions allow for the development of **objectives**, which are more rigidly defined statements supporting the mission.

- **Organizational goals** are specific statements, based on timelines and specific to a particular objective, which in turn supports a mission statement which supports the vision which meets the philosophical needs of the community.

- Social work professionals understand that the vehicle used for the delivery of services and the implementation of inno-

vations required to assist an ever changing multi-racial, multi-cultural, multi-lingual, and automated society is typical of the human service organization.

- Human services organizations are typically charged with the mission of developing services for specific needs experienced by a community or particular clients and providing those services through the use of skilled professionals (or in the case of self-groups, through the use of experienced and concerned individuals).

- A *social work administrator* needs to be sensitive to local, city, county, state, and federal politics, legislation, services needs, and resources.

- Social work administrators must understand small and large organizational dynamics and creation, implementation, and evaluation of policy and procedures. They must possess a working knowledge of the skills required by staff to perform specific tasks, thus ensuring that the most appropriate services are delivered.

- Social work administrators must have strong interpersonal skills. Administration requires leadership and a fundamental understanding of the needs of the community or client to be served and of the skills necessary for staff to ensure quality services.

- *Administrative structures* are defined boundaries whereby professionals function and perform their activities.

- Administrative structures are best described by *organizational flow charts*, useful in understanding the role, power, and authority possessed by persons in the organization.

- Organizational flow charts, which provide a perspective as to the importance of particular services, are useful in ensuring that communications among staff are organized and directed toward accomplishing the mission of the organization.

- In most organizations, *administrative structures* consist of top management, middle management, and on-line staff.

- **Top management** is generally concerned with making decisions, acquiring information from staff or other professionals to make decisions, and the type and quality of services delivered.

- Top management also tends to deal with budget utilization, acquisition of additional or diverse funds, and ensuring that the organization is consistent in program development and evaluation.

- **Middle management** is generally interested in acquiring information to be used or disseminated to top management.

- Middle management tends to supervise a number of program areas and make decisions regarding program integration, staff functions, and future planning.

- **On-line staff** tend to be dedicated to implementing skills which improve the state of the client, meeting the needs of the supervisor or director, and accomplishing the mission of the organization.

- Once administrative structures and staff functions have been defined, it is important that staff be placed in strategic locations to ensure that the appropriate efforts for the delivery of particular services are made.

- Administrative structures, staff functions, and staff roles are the major ingredients in the organization of activity within a human services organization.

- **Evaluation** of social services programs is a major social work administrative function.

- Program evaluation includes the identification or creation of an organization or program's mission, objectives, and goals.

- Program evaluation includes the assessment of an agency's ability to meet mission, objectives, and goals.

- Program evaluation includes the assessment of an agency's processes for collecting data for demonstrating the accomplishment of the agency.

- Program evaluation includes the assessment of agencies' expected results (outcome evaluations).

- Program evaluation includes the identification of variables or factors to be reviewed to ensure that a program is consistent and routine.

- Program evaluation involves connecting social work practice and research by using research methods to improve the efficiency and effectiveness of social programs and the quality of social work services.

- Program evaluation lies in the interface between the delivery of social services and research.

- Program evaluation's primary purpose is to use scientific thinking, methods, measurements, and analysis to improve the effectiveness, efficiency, and quality of social programs.

- Program evaluation is designed to systematically collect programming data based on a set of standards or guidelines.

- Program evaluation is designed to systematically rate the effectiveness and efficiency of services provided.

- Program evaluation is designed to determine whether services comply with mandated expectations of adequate and complete services to consumers.

- Program evaluation is designed to correct any observed deficiencies identified in the process.

- Program evaluation addresses professionally determined standards of services and includes a continuous monitoring program for further evaluation and corrective action.

- *Performance audits and accreditation reviews* are related to program evaluation, although they are derived from different intellectual roots and use different data collecting and analysis methodologies.

- Program evaluation focuses on improving the quality of social programs through social science research methods.

- Performance audits focus on organizational control and accountability issues through accountancy procedures.

- Programs tend to be evaluated against a predetermined, externally derived set of standards devised by bodies with external authority, such as government agencies and professional associations.

- Program evaluation focuses on such issues as the necessary professional composition of the staff, program or services integrity, administrative management, innovations in services, and meeting the needs of the clients.

- Program evaluation may consist of a review of all program components for the purpose of making global recommendations for the overall management and administration of services, future funding, and services to be delivered.

- Comprehensive program evaluation takes into account ideas from as many interested parties as possible through interviews or small-group meetings.

- Often program evaluation consists of a review team reviewing the administrative, budgetary, and programming functions for a specific agency or service delivery system.

- Depending on the depth of the evaluation, focus groups may be helpful in formulating problems for further program evaluations.

- Social work professionals are constantly developing social programs depending on the needs of their clients.

- In general, programs developed for social agencies to implement are based on a formal *community needs assessment*.

- Social programs are developed as a result of expressed need by special groups or identification by governmental, religious, political, or educational entities of groups that have a need.

- *Program development* is at the core of social work practice.

- The *major parameters in program development* are establishing program structures, services, functions, and staff roles.

- **Program structures** include such areas as lines of authority, communication or informational exchange practices, administrative pecking order, areas of responsibility, and management of resources.

- Parameters regarding **service functions** are articulated in the program's vision, mission, objectives, and goals.

- **Staff roles** establish what type of professionals will be providing the services.

- Most social agencies operate within a traditional administrative model.

- Recently in business and even in some social agencies, attempts have been made to move to decentralized models of management, often called **matrix models.**

- The driving philosophical force behind the matrix models of management is the belief that rapid change demands a new flexibility in the administration of any organization.

- **Social program development** involves an organized process for implementation of a set of services to assist in the elimination of a social problem.

- **Research** is an important component of the social work profession.

- Social work research is engaging in a scientific adventure with a set of plans that employs a specific methodology for the study of research hypotheses or questions derived from theory or practice.

- Research is needed by Social Workers for making decisions regarding what interventions are most effective, given a particular situation, concern, or problem.

- Social work administrators are served by research when they attempt to assess the effectiveness of programs, understand the clientele which they serve, or assess the effectiveness of a particular program or intervention over time.

- **Experimental research** is primarily interested in studying the influence of a variable on other variables; therefore, control of the influencing variable is paramount.

- The primary reason for use of an **experimental design** is to test cause and effect. The experimental design tests the hypothesis: "If this, then that" or that the presence or manipulation of A causes B.

- **Randomization** assures that subjects have an equal chance of being assigned to either the experimental or a control group. Randomization procedures strengthen causal findings.

- The primary reason for use of a **quasi-experimental design**, like the experimental design, is to test for cause and effect. Research results based on quasi-experimental designs are not as strong as those from an experimental design.

- The **single-subject design** is most widely used by social work researchers. Single-subject design is most often used in clinical situations for the assessment of intervention effectiveness.

- The single-subject design allows for collection of data at both the individual and group level, so Social Workers can study clinical intervention when working with either mode of treatment.

- The single-subject design primarily allows for the evaluation of intervention on a single individual (the subject).

- Since most Social Workers are interested in assessing their clinical effectiveness, they tend to use single-subject design

- Single-subject designs rely on feedback from ongoing data recording to determine when changes in the intervention are to occur.

- Single-subject designs are not strong in proving or disproving of hypotheses.

- Fundamentally, the format for single-subject design is established on the measurement of a stable baseline (A) followed by the introduction of the intervention (B). This is referred to as the AB design.

- The second most used single-subject design is the **reversal design** (withdrawal). This design, referred to as the ABAB design, consists of four experimental conditions: baseline (A); intervention (B); return to baseline (A); and reintroduction of the intervention (B). The strength of the reversal design is in the withdrawal and reintroduction of the intervention.

- Next to experimental design, social work researchers use **survey research design**.

- The major reason for the use of survey research is the collection of a large amount of information.

- Survey research is a systematic fact-gathering procedure in which a specific series of questions is asked, through written or oral questionnaires, of a representative sample of the group being studied, or of the entire population.

- Surveys are one of the least costly methods for collection of data and most commonly used research methods in social work.

- Surveys make it possible for researchers to gather data from a large sample and generalize to a large population.

- For the most part, survey research is used by the Social Worker because it provides large amount of information, allowing for extensive analysis.

- Survey research design doesn't possess the same level of control over the subject as does the experimental design.

- Generally, a survey is sent to a subject through the mail or handed out, and the subject is asked to complete the survey.

- The **longitudinal design's** major emphasis is the repeated testing of the same phenomenon/measurement in subjects over time.

- The strength of the longitudinal design is that Social Workers can study a particular phenomenon over time.

- **Demographic research** is typically used for the collection of data to describe a group, setting, organization, intervention, or environment.

- Demographic data includes such variables such as gender, religion, social class, education, employment, age, or residence.

- Perhaps the largest contribution that social work has made to helping is the concept of **person in situation.**

- The person in situation concept emphasizes that a person be viewed not just in terms of intrapsychic processes, or in terms of illness, but rather as a total being who is impacted by environment.

- It has been suggested that the person in situation approach is more a perspective that guides practice than a practice model.

- The person in situation approach draws on Freudian theory, ego psychology, object relations theory, and self psychology in order to understand human personality and coping abilities.

- The person in situation approach also looks at the adult life cycle; issues impacting on women; issues of divorce and sexual abuse; gay and lesbian development; cultural, ethnic and racial diversity; and the impact of personality on functioning.

- The relationship between the client and the Social Worker is the vehicle for helping in this approach.

- **Person in environment** is a system of classification that utilizes social work's unique approach to the total person in describing the problems of social functioning of adult clients.

- **Confidentiality** is a principle of social work ethics whereby the Social Worker may not disclose information about a client without the client's permission.

- Information generally considered to be confidential includes the client's identity, content of professional discussions, professional opinions about the client, and data in the clinical record.

- **Absolute confidentiality** supports the proposition that no information about a client shall be disclosed to others, regardless of circumstances.

- **Relative confidentiality** supports the proposition that, under certain circumstances, Social Workers may ethically disclose information about a client.

- The best description of confidentiality in the arena of social work is found in the **National Association of Social Workers Code of Ethics.**

- Respect for the client as a person and for the client's right to privacy underlies the Social Worker-client relationship.

- In dealing with youth, although assurance of confidentiality enhances the relationship and the willingness of the young person to develop and adhere to a case plan, the young client should be advised that there are circumstances in which confidentiality cannot be maintained.

- A 1976 ruling by the Supreme Court of California, **Tarasoff v. Regents,** states that, under certain circumstances, psychotherapists whose clients tell them that they intend to harm someone are obliged to warn the intended victim.

- Some Social Workers argue that the effect of the Tarasoff v. Regents ruling is to make it more difficult for therapists to assure their clients of confidentiality and for clients to express certain hostile feelings to their therapists.

- In June 1996, the United States Supreme Court ruled **(Jaffe v. Redmond)** that conversations between Clinical Social Workers and their clients are protected from disclosure in federal trials.

- During recent years, **empowerment** of self, clients, governments, cultural groups, social groups, organizations, families, wives, Social Workers, agencies, communities, minority groups, and students has been a major factor in social work practice.

- Empowerment includes exchange of information and a consciousness-raising process which enables either the Social Worker or the client to problem solve, exert leadership, and increase decision-making influence.

- Empowerment is based on the ideal of employing the strengths of the individual or group encouraging advocacy. The goal of empowerment is to increase the individual's skill, thus improving his or her means of obtaining social justice by addressing just distribution of resources.

- Empowerment helps professional Social Workers to acquire an equitable distribution of resources and influence among different groups in society.

- Empowerment results from successful social action carried out jointly by clients and Social Workers (or by clients alone, when they are ready and interested) and is emphasized in life-modeled practice.

- The areas of *loss and grief* are coming more into focus in social work.

- Because people are living longer, they have more opportunity to experience loss at varying levels. The profession of social work must devote more energy to the delivery of service in the areas of nursing home care, chronic illness, post traumatic stress, mental illness, and neonatal intensive care.

- *Grief* is an intense and acute sorrow resulting from loss. It has many of the same symptoms as physical or mental illness, although it tends to diminish with time. Like all illnesses, grief can end in complete or partial recovery.

- *Grief reaction* is experienced as a deep sadness resulting from an important loss.

- *Grief work* is a series of emotional stages or phases following an important loss, which gradually permit adjustment and recovery.

- Loss and grief have been human concerns for hundreds of years.

- Attitudes toward bereavement have been influenced by multiple variables such as culture, circumstances surrounding the death, and age of the lost one.

- Scientific study of bereavement did not begin until the 1940s.

- Numerous grief researchers and theoreticians have proposed varied conceptualizations to explain normal and complicated grief.

- Elisabeth Kübler-Ross is best known for her classic *On Death and Dying*. Kübler-Ross's concepts of death and dying assisted in understanding the cognitive and psychological movement of the patient along the path to death. Kübler-Ross's concepts also have been applied to people suffering losses other than death, such as the loss of a body part or a degenerative condition that leads to progressive physical deterioration.

- ***Human behavior*** can be thought of as:

    1) a result of thoughts and emotions, based on perceptions

    2) a result of past learned methods for dealing with situations

    3) at times psychotic (mental disorder — organic or psychological in origin)

    4) based on social and genetic variables

    5) based on past experiences

    6) changeable

    7) directed to getting psychological and physical needs met

    8) in one's control

    9) structured by cultural expectations and norms

    10) not random

    11) organized

    12) predictable

    13) purposeful

    14) self-serving (information is sought to support one's own values and attitudes)

    15) structured to meet basic needs.

- Major areas to be considered for further understanding of behavior include perceptions, values, attitudes, and beliefs.

- Individuals acquire their *perceptions and values* from information in their environment and their experiences. They seek information which supports their values, attitudes, and beliefs and organize information into categories which make sense of the world.

- *Psychotherapy* involves the use of a professional relationship along with a strategic approach to study, change, or enhance existing thoughts, emotions and behavior.

- The psychotherapeutic process involves dealing with fears, defenses, expectations, and past socialization with the mission of engaging in change for improved social functioning.

- A major contribution made by Freud was the concept of *defense mechanism.*

- A defense mechanism is a mental process that protects the personality from anxiety, guilt feelings, or unacceptable thoughts.

- Defense mechanisms, as used in psychoanalytic theory, are the ego's protective methods of reducing anxiety by unconsciously distorting reality.

- *Avoidance* is a defense mechanism resembling denial, involving refusal to face certain situations or objects because they present unconscious impulses or punishments for those impulses.

- *Compensation* is a defense mechanism which involves an effort to make up for imaginary or real behaviors that are considered undesirable.

- *Conversion* is a defense mechanism which involves the transfer of anxiety or emotional conflict to overt physical manifestations or symptoms such as pain, loss of feeling, or paralysis.

- *Denial* is a defense mechanism which protects the personality from anxiety or guilt by disavowing or ignoring unacceptable thoughts, emotions, or wishes.

- **Displacement** is a defense mechanism which reduces anxiety experienced with specific thoughts or emotions by transferring them to another thought or emotion that is more acceptable or tolerable.

- **Idealization** is a defense mechanism which involves overestimation of another person attributes.

- **Intellectualization** is a defense mechanism in which the person ignores emotions and analyzes problems or conflicts objectively.

- **Overcompensation** is a defense mechanism which includes an effort to engage in counterbalancing a real or imagined deficiency.

- **Rationalization** is a defense mechanism by which a person justifies a behavior or thought to make it acceptable when it is unacceptable at a deeper psychological level.

- **Substitution** is a defense mechanism which involves replacing an unattainable or unacceptable objective with one that is attainable and acceptable.

- Social Workers commonly use **supportive therapy** when assisting their clients.

- Hidden in the concept of supportive therapy is the belief that individuals, given support can, solve their issues and make healthy life choices.

- **Supportive services** have a huge impact in family preservation. Spend some time looking at this form of practice as you prepare for the examination.

- Supportive therapy is very much a part of work with the elderly and in clinical practice with the chronically mentally ill.

- Supportive therapy is an important part of medical social work

- Supportive therapy emphasizes helping the individual develop, maintain, and monitor more effective and appropriate behaviors, emotions, and cognition.

- Social Workers who use supportive therapy employ interventions which include reassurance, and identification of the client's strengths.

- Supportive therapy does not typically delve into the unconscious

- Early models of social work practice evolved without any connection to formal theories of human behavior and personality.

- With the exception of the Rankian schools (Penn. and UNC), the profession adopted the psychoanalytical developmental theory as a basis for understanding personality.

- *Freud* suggested the following **structure of personality**: id, ego, and superego.

- Freud thought that the **libido** (sexual energy) was the primary motivator for behavior.

- Freud believed that the early years of life were the most important to the understanding of adult behavior.

- Freud suggested *five stages of maturation*: oral, anal, phallic, latency, and genital.

- Freud believed that the major tasks of development were completed by the end of the phallic stage.

- Freud taught that each stage had specific developmental tasks and further suggested that every stage was difficult because of the conflict between the id and ego.

- Freud believed that individuals could become stuck at a stage if the main developmental work was not accomplished during that stage.

- *Erickson* specialized in working with children.

- Erickson added culture and society as important contributors to personality development.

- Erickson viewed personality as developing throughout the individual's life cycle.

- Erickson's model of life includes eight stages of development, each with its own crisis.

- According to Erickson an individual's tasks are to achieve trust, autonomy, initiative, competence, identity, generativity (or productivity), integrity, and acceptance.

- In the 1970s and 1980s cognitive and learning theorists merged the two approaches into *cognitive-behavioral theory*, one of the most widely used practice models in current times.

- *Cognitive theory* is interested in how individuals perceive, remember, think, and make use of language.

- In the profession of social work, roles play an important part in the assessment of individuals and groups.

- *Roles* are a set of culturally determined patterns of behavior prescribed for an individual who occupies a specific status.

- *Role theory* is a set of concepts, based on sociocultural and anthropological investigations, which pertain to the way people are influenced in their behaviors by the social positions they hold and the expectations accompanying those positions.

- Role theory includes such ideas such as what social norm is attached to a given social position and how that influences the behavior of others.

- Role theory is useful in social work because it allows for a comprehensive understanding of others' behavior.

- *Systems theory* is an organized body of knowledge that attempts to explain some aspect of reality in a manner that may be verified in an empirical manner.

- Social work has moved from having very little practice theory to having at least twenty major theoretical systems shaping current practice.

- In the early days the *psychosocial approach* drew from psychodynamic theory as well as social role theory.

- The *problem-solving approach* emphasizes the importance of social support, cognitive processes, and participatory democracy.

- In the 1950s *family systems theory* came to the fore and provided a bridge between group and case work.

- In social work, *ecological theory* is an orientation that looks at the interaction of individuals and their environment.

- Concepts in this approach include adaptation, transactions, goodness of fit between people and their environments, reciprocity, and mutuality. When interventions are attempted, they focus on the interface between the individual (or other client group, family, or community) and the environment.

- *General systems theory* has been described as an attempt to explain in a holistic manner the behavior of societies and people by identifying the components of the system that interact and the controls that keep these subsystems stable and in a state of equilibrium.

- The general system theory approach addresses issues of boundaries, roles, and relationships, as well as the way information travels from one portion of the system to another.

- *Family system theory* emphasizes the reciprocal relationships and mutual influences between individuals and the whole.

- The *empathic model* encourages the implementation of interventions and skills which assist in the creation of a positive working professional relationship between the Social Worker and the client.

- The major principle of the empathic model is the emphasis on the worker's ability to develop a positive and professional working relationship with the client.

- The empathic model is based on positive regard for the client, non-judgmental statements, and non-passive warmth.

- An *inter-organizational collaboration* is a group of independent organizations committed to working together toward a common goal while maintaining their basic independence.

- An **interdisciplinary collaboration** is the bringing together of individuals from different educational disciplines to provide a service or solve the problems of a client. An example might be a hospital-based child protection team.

- Any **collaboration** is a group process and as such is subject to the process issues that occur when individuals or organizations are brought together.

- The roots of collaboration can be found in systems or ecologically based social work practice models.

- A collaboration begins by bringing together the collaborators and mobilizing them.

- A group may cease collaboration because a goal has been met (or it hasn't) or because the needs of the client group have changed.

- Some collaborations move from informal to formal.

- Social Workers have become far more aware of the impact of **culture** on practice in recent years.

- A heightened focus on environment, which began in the 1970s, has sparked an interest in using understandings of culturally specific populations to create appropriate practice standards and modalities.

- Social Workers recognize that clients are impacted by the status of their cultural group, which in turn influences their opportunities in life and their life-styles.

- The **impact of minority status** on clients, including issues of stratification, stereotyping, and systemic entrapment are critical social work issues.

- Social Workers now must look for new ways of practicing with people of color, women, gay men, and lesbians, as well as groups who struggle with issues such as AIDS.

- **Psychotherapy** is the bringing to awareness and manipulation of emotional and cognitive states by self or others.

- **Clinical work** is a major aspect of social work.

- **Basic social work values and attitudes** are the concepts that human beings strive to be honest to self, in control of self, in control of destiny, and in control of their behavior.

- Social work services are supported by values and ideals which suggest that interventions lead to client well-being as a result of learning about self, acquiring awareness of personal needs, reducing the number of defense mechanisms, and accepting life as ambiguous.

- A critical aspect of social work practice is the comprehensive collection of relevant information regarding the client's history.

- Relevant **assessment information** must be collected to ensure that the problem identification process leads to the selection of the client's most important concern.

- The **initial assessment** must include collection of information about the mental status of the client, physical appearance, precipitating factors, fundamental family information, and demographic data.

- The initial assessment must include such data as the client's perception of the problem and potential goal to be accomplished in resolving the concern.

- **Psychosocial assessment** is the Social Worker's major method for the collection, integration, and prioritizing of historical client data for the purpose of treatment planning, diagnostics, understanding the client's social and psychological functioning, and appraisal of the treatment process.

- Psychosocial assessment includes the Social Worker's summary judgment of the problem to be solved, results derived from psychological tests, legal status, brief descriptive expressions of the problem configuration, a description of existing assets and resources, the prognosis or prediction of the outcome, and the plan designed to resolve the problem.

- The psychosocial assessment includes both historical and current information regarding family composition, health status, employment, education, marital status, economic status, reli-

gious preference, sexual preference, and drug and alcohol use or abuse,

■ Acquiring the relevant information is part of the process of developing a rational plan for assisting the client.

■ Information obtained in the psychosocial study is used to arrive at the psychosocial assessment, treatment plan, and diagnostic statement.

■ The *history of social work* can be found in the development of ideas about assessment over the years.

■ Mary Richmond created the concept of *social diagnosis*.

■ As the profession has changed over the years in terms of emphasis, so has the emphasis on assessment.

■ The end of World War I pushed Social Workers into the treatment of returning soldiers who suffered from what was then called "shell shock."

■ The content of any assessment is determined by the setting in which it takes place.

■ One of the issues in assessment is the fact that Social Workers are frequently the first line of defense for clients in need of *immediate medical attention*.

■ In addition to assessing the need for immediate medical attention, Social Workers often have to assess *suicide potential*.

■ While Social Workers are not physicians and make no medical determinations, they can do much to help clients seek medical help for issues that do not seem to have another explanation.

■ The steps in any assessment remain the same no matter what the focus of the assessment: collection of data, interpretation of the data, evaluation of the client's functioning and the resources available to the client, problem specification, and treatment planning.

- Given the stress on providing more service at less cost, Social Workers can expect to be faced with more demand for *crisis intervention*.

- *Crisis intervention theory*, with roots running back to the 1940s, '50s and '60s, is based primarily on a synthesis of ego and cognitive psychology and individual stress theories.

- *Situational stress* generally causes individuals to experience acute emotional and social imbalance.

- Situational stress may not be pathological. It is likely to happen to all of us in our lifetimes, when we experience life events we consider devastating, such as divorce, death of a loved one, or losing a job.

- Individuals who experience a life imbalance because of a crisis will work to regain balance.

- While struggling to regain the necessary emotional balance, the individual will be emotionally vulnerable for a period of time.

- During times of crisis, individuals may be more susceptible to psychological interventions.

- No matter what the crisis, individuals experience similar stages of psychological or social responses.

- Individual psychological growth and development can result from crisis, as can negative outcomes.

- Crisis may be created by situations such as death of a loved one or serious illness, and by developmental or evolutionary issues such as adolescence, divorce, and retirement.

- Research and literature in the area of crisis intervention present a characterization of the crisis state as severe emotional distress, followed by feelings of depression, anger, confusion, anxiety, and disorganization.

- Crisis has the potential to enhance the coping ability of clients.

- **Crisis intervention** is different from other brief treatments.

- Crisis intervention tends to focus on coping dysfunctions where there is a clear precipitant event.

- Crisis intervention focuses on emotional issues.

- Preparation for the **first interview** should include reviewing any information that may be at hand regarding the client, including records from any previous contacts.

- The interviewer must be sensitive to the information brought by the client.

- A **positive relationship** includes feelings of respect, warmth, and understanding.

- The middle phase of the interview has been called the working section.

- During an interview, data gathering does not mean simply asking questions; it also means understanding behavior exhibited by the client.

- During an interview, simply sitting quietly can create important space for the client.

- Help offered should relate to the presenting problem, not deeper issues or other things that the interviewer may feel important

- Trust is key to the acceptance of the offer of help.

- One reality of the professional interview is that it must end.

- The best ending for an interview comes with the agreement of the client.

- **Medical social work** occurs in hospitals, health care settings, prison infirmaries, and mental health and medical clinics.

- The major mission of the Medical Social Worker is to facilitate and advocate good health, prevent illness, and help ill clients resolve social and psychological problems related to their illness.

- Social work in health began in the community with agencies that focused on public health problems such as tuberculosis, syphilis, polio, and unmarried pregnancy.

- The American Association of Hospital Social Workers came into existence in the early part of this century.

- In the mid 1920s the American Hospital Association produced the first formulation of medical social work.

- The original function of medical social work was to work with social problems that interfered with the client's plan for medical care.

- During the 1950s and '60s, medical social work grew and expanded, becoming more professional, developing greater interest in research, and demanding higher technical skills.

- *Diagnosis related groups* (DRGs) were established under the Deficit Reduction Act of 1984.

- This shifted the responsibility of acute care from third-party payers to providers of service. Length of stay became crucial because hospitals could lose money on stays that exceeded the DRG allotment and could make money on brief stays. Although DRGs affected federal programs such as Medicare and Medicaid, insurance carriers were quick to adopt them as benchmarks for measuring length of stay.

- State legislatures and the federal government have responded to patient complaints with new legislation that seeks to protect patient rights.

- In this rapidly changing environment, the Medical Social Worker must take into account, the hospital system, environment, family systems, social systems, and community

- Medical Social Workers deal with individuals and the family, participate in multi-disciplinary teams, identify or arrange community resources, help with grief and mourning, identify potential neglect and abuse, and deal with the ethical stresses that come with cost-driven care.

- Medical Social Workers should possess skills in crisis management, psychosocial assessment, psychological review, service and intervention planning, brief counseling, bereavement counseling, discharge planning, group work, emergency services, record keeping, and aftercare services.

- The major objective for the Social Worker is to understand the client, the client's social environment, and the integration of the client's needs with his social environment.

- Good medical social work practice is to begin the process of discharge planning at time of intake.

- Group work by Medical Social Workers is becoming more a standard of practice because of the need to keep costs down and to provide more services to a larger group of clients.

- Medical Social Workers will continue to experience change as the profession struggles with the political issues that are part of today's health care environment.

- The number of **at-risk children** can be expected to increase for the foreseeable future, especially those children who because of family violence, drug abuse, gang affiliation, and poverty are not effectively using existing educational resources.

- *School Social Workers* will be challenged with increased dropout rates, especially among minority children, and a social system which has not yet realized that prioritizing the education of children is a major societal value. Currently, the focus on student' rights and cultural diversity has led to involvement in school, family, and community efforts by Social Workers.

- *School Social Workers* are today the point at which many families come into contact with the social services system. The values that guide school social work are much like those that impact all of social work, such as client self-determination and beginning where the client is.

- In providing for the child, School Social Workers include all stakeholders in the situation, including the student, the family, the community, the teachers, and principal.

- The **traditional school social work model** gives special attention to individual children who are experiencing social, emotional, or physical problems that prevent them from adequately functioning within a school setting.

- Social Workers who use the traditional school social work model serve as a support system or provide consultation to both the family and school.

- The **school change model** emphasizes institutional change with the aim of altering conditions within a school setting.

- School Social Workers who employ the school change model become involved with administrators and teachers to change conditions that have a negative influence on children.

- The **systems model** in the practice of school social work includes dealing with the student's needs and working to change the school, family, and community.

- School Social Workers interact with school administrators and teachers and provide feedback to other professionals such as school nurses and school psychologists.

- School social work practice touches on resource development.

- **Case management functions** include staying in touch with the comprehensive needs of the client, linking the client to the services, and monitoring the services offered to make sure that they work well for the client.

- The profession of social work makes heavy demands on the use of interviewing techniques for the purpose of assisting individuals and groups.

- At all levels of social work, from the Baccalaureate to the Doctorate, the clinical interview is the most used and the most valued tool among Social Workers.

- The **imposed and un-imposed interview** are widely used by Social Workers.

- The **imposed interview** requires that the Social Worker be sensitive to the client's unwillingness to engage in a positive working clinical relationship.

- The imposed interview requires that the Social Worker be aware that resistance, anger, frustration, and unwillingness to share are the major areas of challenge in an interview setting.

- A fundamental challenge for the Social Worker is to engage the client in a nonthreatening manner; to slowly, with the client, define the areas that may be of value to explore; and to develop a clinical contract surrounding those issues which appear to be nonthreatening to the client.

- The clinical relationship, along with empathy and sensitivity to the needs of the client, will outweigh the client's resistance to treatment.

- Clinical Social Workers know that the Tarasoff decision in California creates a *"duty to warn"* third parties who may be the object of a client's intent to do bodily harm.

- Social Workers also have, as of June 1996, a much more complete therapist privilege.

- Social work ethics are clear about the need to protect clients from intrusions into their private lives.

- Some Social Workers are deeply distressed about the requirements of managed care to share very personal information in order to get benefits.

- A Social Worker has the absolute responsibility to involve the client in the process of **problem identification.**

- Identifying the client's problem is a prerequisite to implementing a treatment model.

- Clients usually can define the target problem.

- There must be congruence between the client's perception of the problem and the practitioner's determination of the focus of treatment.

- *Psychoanalytic theories* seek core interpersonal issues.

- *Cognitive-behavioral theories* focus on the present, on goal-oriented interventions, on what is wrong. They seek to replace unwanted cognition or behaviors.

- No field of practice is changing more rapidly or has greater potential for growth than that of **work with adults**.

- The **life cycle** is the age-related sequence of changes and systematic development that a person experiences between birth and death.

- It is human nature to want some order and predictability in the constantly changing life that we each experience.

- The numbers of individuals in the rapidly aging Boomer generation will impact the demand for services.

- Social roles are a frequently discussed concept in relation to aging.

- The concept of social roles describes society's expectations for people in particular social positions.

- Study of the adult life cycle requires review of the biological, psychological, sociological, anthropological, and historical perspectives.

- Although writers differ as to when certain life cycle issues occur, they agree that there are certain things that we must all go through: separation from family of origin, development of a personal vision, recognition of failure to achieve all of our dreams, increase in generativity, and then losses that are a part of aging, including physical and mental changes.

- About 5% of the population past the age of 65 suffer from **dementia** that interferes with cognitive functioning either moderately or severely. Another 10% have a mild cognitive impairment.

- **Alzheimer's disease** affects half of those with severe intellectual impairment.

- **Multi-infarct dementia** occurs when blood clots repeatedly cut off the supply to the brain, often in the form of small strokes. Multi-infarct dementia causes about 20% of the deaths from chronic organic brain dysfunction and is present in 12% of Alzheimer's patients.

- *Parkinson's disease* may appear as early as the thirties.

- *Clinical depression* is often missed or mistaken for an organic dysfunction when dealing with the elderly.

- Social Workers are expected to deal with the social issues that relate to aging.

- Women make up 72% of the adults in poverty.

- One of the often neglected issues with the elderly is the question of *suicide.*

- Suicide attempts by people under the age of 35 fail more often than they succeed, but people over the age of 50 are more likely to succeed.

- *Social isolation* seems to play a part in the suicide attempts of older people who are depressed.

- Women tend to suffer from **hypochondriasis**, which peaks between ages 60-64.

- *Hispanics* are a diverse group, each subgroup having distinctive cultural elements.

- Mexican-Americans place a strong value on family, family ties, and the use of the extended family for child rearing.

- A major element in the Mexican-American family is the great respect directed toward the elderly.

- **Native Americans** comprise more than 400 different tribal groups and speak more than 250 different languages.

- There are four major groups of Native Americans: reservation, rural, migrant, and urban.

- Some statistics indicates that 71% of elderly Native Americans experience difficulty with daily activities.

- Most research suggests that **Asian Americans** tend to be a part of a tightly knit community where membership is close and strong supportive relationships exist with children and grandchildren.

- Recent research suggests that among second- and third-generation Asian Americans, the obligation to support the elderly seems to be waning and many elderly live within ethnic enclaves in urban areas, depending on non-relatives.

- The Social Worker must choose the **intervention method** that seems most appropriate to the client and the system.

- The wise Social Worker will always maximize the resources in the environment. This can be especially helpful with those clients who are poor, isolated, or young.

- *Family therapy* is a social and intellectual movement as well as a technique for helping.

- Feminist thinkers have contributed a great deal to recent thinking about family systems, breaking down stereotypes of role expectations.

- Family therapists have begun to struggle with the notion that family comes in many different structures, with different values and norms.

- Unlike some other therapies, family therapy continues to grow and change.

- In the mid-1980s there was a rapid increase in *family preservation* and other family support services.

- The underlying belief of the family preservation movement is that many children could remain safely at home if services were provided intensively and early.

- The shift to family preservation represents a movement to an ecological perspective that sees the environment as both the source of and solution to problems.

- The passage of the **Adoption Assistance and Child Welfare Act of 1980** (PL. 96-272) was a major factor in the development of the family preservation approach.

- Child Welfare League standards recommend low caseloads of two to six families.

- Emphasis on active listening, engagement with the client, and implied respect for the client's ability to change, all relate back to *functional theory*.

- *Group practice* began in the settlement house movement in the late 19th century.

- By the 1930s group work was becoming recognized as a professional approach to helping.

- The 1970s brought sensitivity groups, encounter groups, transactional analysis, behavior modification, psychodrama, and gestalt.

- Group work relies on concepts from social systems theory to describe group functioning.

- All group work, no matter what its perspective, is cognizant of the maintenance and task functions that are necessary to the functioning of the group.

- Group maintenance includes welcoming new members, expressing caring and concern for each other, and using humor as ways of supporting the group.

- Task functions are activities that promote the achievement of goals.

- Group development theories provide a way of looking at issues such as the life span of the group.

- Group composition is the selection and modification of membership in the group.

- Assessment of group function requires ongoing attention to the process of the group: how is the group evolving?

- Group goal setting and contracting may involve individual treatment objectives to issues around the group's functioning.

- More groups tend to be open-ended; therefore adaptation to change presents a challenge to group members and the leader.

- More and more groups are involuntary in nature, so leaders have to work harder to show members where they do have choice.

- *Psychosocial/psychoanalytical theories of child development,* which believe that heredity and environment interact to produce results, focus on social and emotional development.

- *Cognitive/developmental theories of child development* focus on language and cognitive development.

- *Behavioral/social learning theories of child development,* which believe that most learning comes from environmental experiences (specifically history of consequences for behavior), focus on managing specific behaviors.

- *Erickson* focused on the development of the healthy personality as opposed to Freud, who was more interested in the neurotic personality.

- Erickson focused on social and cultural influences on the developing child.

- Erickson believed that as the individual interacts with his environment, he encounters certain psychosocial crises that roughly correspond to certain ages and stages of life.

- Erickson believed that each individual must work through each of these crises in order to develop a healthy ego identity (clarity about and acceptance of self and identification with the culture in which he lives).

- *Sensorimotor Stage:* 0-2 Years — Infants take in information through their senses, process it, and act upon it. This is a coordination of sensory input and motor activities.

- *Preconceptual Stage:* 2-4 years — Ability to use symbols is shown by language pretend play, and drawing. No true concepts formed.

- *Intuitive Stage:* 4-7 years — Ability to manipulate and transform information in basic ways; can form mental representations of objects and events but cannot think by operations.

- *Concrete Operations Stage:* 7-11 years — Ability to understand logical principles that apply to concrete external objects.

- **Formal Operations Stage:** Older than 11 — Ability to think abstractly with the constraints of the immediate situations; can think in terms of possibilities and probabilities.

- **Lawrence Kohlberg's** most interesting work in the area of child development centered on morality.

- Kohlberg argued that individuals move through a number of moral development stages which directly influence the ability of children to engage in specific moral decisions.

- **Preconventional:** 0-9 Years — Morality of self-interest: to avoid punishment or gain concrete rewards.

- **Conventional:** 10-14 Years — Morality of law and social rule: to gain approval or avoid punishment

- **Postconventional:** 14-Adulthood — Morality of abstract principles: to affirm agreed-upon rights and personal ethical principles.

- **Childhood** can be defined as the period in the life cycle between birth and the achievement of complete physical maturation.

- Human development theory makes the point that childhood encompasses not only physical development but also emotional, cognitive, social, and moral development.

- About one fifth of the total population in the U.S. is under 14 years of age.

- There has been a consistent decline in the fertility rate over the last thirty years.

- In 1991 nearly 70% of all children had a working mother.

- African-American mortality rate is twice that of whites and almost as high among other ethnic groups.

- Over half of the African-American and Hispanic students in 1990 performed at less than the basic level.

- The beginning of adolescence for girls is usually considered to be the onset of menstruation, whereas for boys the onset is less clear.

- **Adolescence,** the life cycle period between childhood and adulthood that begins at puberty and ends with young adulthood has at least five stages: preadolescence, early adolescence, middle adolescence, adolescence, and late adolescence.

- **Behavioral theorists** believe that only behavior that can be observed directly can be understood and explained.

- **Skinner** believed that behavior is understood only by examining the consequences (as consequences control action).

- **Social learning theory** grew out of behavioral theory.

- **Piaget** theorized that the concrete operational thinking of the child becomes qualitatively different in the formal operations of the adolescent because the adolescent can consider possibilities, manipulate mental constructs, and assess probabilities.

- **Preadolescence** is characterized by the need for intimacy that is expressed through strong relationships, usually with people of the same sex.

- With the changes of **puberty** comes the shift to intimate relationships with people of the opposite sex, or perhaps of the same sex, patterned on early same-sex relationships.

- The greatest need for friendships for girls occurs in **middle adolescence,** when there is a keen dread of rejection and isolation.

- Surveys of adolescent sexual behavior have shown rates of **condom use** that ranges from 2.1% to 38%.

- Twenty-five percent of those with **sexually transmitted diseases** are adolescents.

- Since 1988 there has been an 84% increase overall in the rate of reported cases of AIDS among adolescents. The rate of increase for girls alone in the same time period is 119%.

- Though adolescents make up only a small part of the total number of AIDS patients, their rate of increase is a great concern.

- Between 1972 and 1989, the rate rose from 13.5 per thousand to 17.4 per thousand in 1989 for teens 14 years or younger, and from 64.1 per thousand to 74.9 per thousand in teens 15 to 17 years old.

- While young mothers chose adoption in the 1960s, only 10% of current teens place their babies for adoption.

- In 1990, 20% of first births in the white population were to adolescents.

- Trends in the use of drugs by adolescents show an increase from the mid-1970s to 1982 and a slow reduction since then.

- *Alcohol* is the drug of choice and the drug most frequently abused by the adolescent population.

- Alcohol use decreased among 12- to 17-year-olds between the late 1980s and the early 1990s.

- Some studies indicate a strong relationship between alcohol-related social problems and school misconduct, especially for males.

- A *runaway youth* is an individual under 18 years of age who is away from home at least overnight without permission.

- Runaway statistics for the 1990s show that between 1.3 million and 1.5 million children run away per year.

- The *four types of runaways* are those who are running away from something (family problems, sexual abuse), those who have been thrown out by their parents, those who are running toward something, and social isolates who have been abandoned by their family.

- *Suicide* follows only accidents and homicides as the leading cause of death in adolescents.

- The rate of suicide is notably higher for males than for females.

- Factors in youthful suicide include dysfunctional and conflicted families, divorce, separation, and death of a parent.

- A basic understand of the *life cycle* is necessary to acquire a sense of human maturation.

- *Ages 16-18:* Escape from dominance, marked by a struggle to escape from parental dominance.

- *Age 18-22:* Leaving the family: The majority of individuals break away from their families in their early 20s.

- *Age 22-28:* Building a workable life: The trend in the mid-20s is to seek mastery of the real world.

- *Age 29-34:* Crisis of questions: At the heart of this crisis is a serious questioning of what life is all about.

- *Age 35-43:* Crisis of urgency: Individuals age 35 to 43 are typically becoming more aware of the reality of death.

- *Age 43-50:* Attaining stability: In the late 40s, acceptance of one's fate takes hold.

- *Age 50 and up:* Mellowing: After 50 there is a noticeable mellowing with emphasis on sharing day-to-day joys and sorrows.

- *Community change* is the end result of social energies which promote movement toward social evolution and development.

- Community change is critical in building more progressive communities.

- Community change, like small group change, is generally preceded by a condition of conflict because of the need for ordered change to occur.

- Social work was based on the need to provide a sense of community in the newly mobile industrial society.

- *Social planning* refers to community organization, community development, program development, social policy analysis, program implementation, and strategic management planning.

- *Services* are offered to provide people with the things which they need to survive, develop, and succeed in society.

- **Advocacy** is based on the idea that if people are suffering, it is not simply the fault of the sufferers, but society itself has problems and needs change.

- Advocacy can promote legislative or administrative change, and legal action is often a part of the process.

- Advocates always represent someone else, with the typical goal of social justice.

- In most human service agencies, the supervising Social Worker is responsible for the direction, management, and administration of staff members.

- **Supervision of professional Social Workers** is performed in order to develop, implement, and evaluate the possible service to the client.

- Supervision focuses on the development of skills directed toward professional practice.

- A core goal of supervision is to develop and evolve as a professional and to share social work knowledge and skills.

- Supervision is an active process in which the supervisor shares information and the supervisee applies the information in a real setting.

- **Advocacy** is a fundamental principle and activity within the profession of social work. Advocacy has taken a significant place in social work and remains a core component of social work practice.

- Advocacy, like empowerment, suggests that individuals, communities, and groups will become more productive if assisted to acquire resources and a sense of influence over their world.

- Advocacy, involves assisting, defending, supporting, or suggesting a set of strategic actions to deal with unmet needs, social problems, or social injustice, in the hope of acquiring and enjoying social justice.

- Case management, in general, involves the identification, location, and implementation of resources for the empowerment of the individual, community, or group.

- Advocacy may include community organization or supporting specific legislation, political positions, or administrative decisions which are considered to bring about social change.

- Social Workers who are interested in advocacy must understand the dynamics and political realities of the situation and the public perception of the issues specific to the defined problem for which advocacy is desired.

- A method for structuring and implementing an advocacy intervention is to undertake a comprehensive assessment of environmental factors contributing to the perceived injustice and to create a plan for strategically intervening and directly creating change in the environment.

- Clinical Social Workers are prime targets for suit as a result of their independent practice, but agency workers no longer are as protected by the concepts of sovereign immunity or charitable immunity as they once were.

- In today's world there is a greater emphasis on troubled relationships with clients. The allegations in order of frequency were the following: 1) exploiting the client for personal advantage; 2) deceit, dishonesty, or fraud; 3 & 4) a tie between failure to exercise professional and impartial judgement, and condoning or engaging in multiple relationships with clients; 5) withdrawal of services without regard to the client's need; 6) failure to serve clients with devotion or loyalty; 7) mishandling of termination; 8) failure to create conditions that facilitated competent practice by colleagues; 9) unfair evaluation of other staff members; 10) exploiting professional relationships for personal gain; and 11) failure to treat colleagues with respect and fairness.

- Licensing boards report that **boundary violations** are the most common reasons for action against a Social Worker.

- The most obvious ethical violation is **sexual relations with a client**.

- Another ethical violation that needs to be watched is **financial boundary violations**.

- More professions are reporting dual relationships in which the professional and the client go into business together, or perhaps the professional borrows money from the client.

- *Malpractice* is professional negligence or misconduct.

- Negligence means that by a professional act of **commission** or an act of **omission** the client is injured by the Social Worker.

- About a fifth of all complaints involve sexual misconduct.

- A sexual relationship with a client can never be considered to be in a client's best interest.

- Many states and federal courts provide Social Workers with the same privilege as attorneys and physicians as well as clergy.

- A Social Worker can be held liable if he fails to warn the appropriate persons that a client intends to do harm to a specific individual.

- A Social Worker can be held liable for not protecting the client from his own self-destructive impulses.

- Social Workers are being given more and more opportunities to educate, no matter what their work setting.

- The primary role of a Social Worker is to create an environment in which the client is able to safely experience growth and development.

- All social work is based on **communication**, the basic tool for relationship building.

- Social work is becoming more interested in the ways in which communication is impacted by culture.

- The stress experienced in society today, children's issues, youth services, and the increasing needs of the elderly have awakened an interest in the concept of **community social work**.

- A fundamental principle of social work is to work with the client or the client's environment to either improve or make possible the ideals of self-empowerment.

- It is clear to many Social Workers that by moving toward or maintaining *self-determinism*, clients may more fully enjoy self growth and development.

- Social Workers must be constantly aware that their values, attitudes, perspectives, and beliefs are not the driving force in the change process.

- The preservation of self-determinism is a constant theme in the practice of social work, for self-determinism sets the stage for change and human evolution.

- Without self-determinism clients will simply not be able to assist themselves as they encounter new or different experiences.

- **Work with adults** is a fast growing field for Social Workers. According to some demographers, the population is increasing most rapidly in the over-85 age range.

- Studies of families where alcoholism is a problem show that they often have characteristics in common such as high levels of cohesion, low levels of expression, high levels of depression, and low levels of independence.

- Studies of the elderly have demonstrated that gender differences among men and women tend to increase with age.

- Social Workers who evaluate their practice tend to use the single subject design.

- The most stringent research design which controls for extraneous variables is experimental research.

- The paradigm most often credited as being created by the social work profession is Social System.

- The three primary symptoms of **Attention Deficit/ Hyperactivity Disorder** are inattention, impulsivity, and over-activity.

- **Supervision**, a central component of social work education and practice, can be described as a tool for the development of professional skills.

- One of the major long-term side-effects of the prolonged use of **lithium** is kidney changes.

- A **statistical mean** is a measure of averages.

- In most cases, development of a **professional helping relationship** is the core of the counseling experience. The empathic approach is useful during the initial phase of a professional helping relationship.

- The **service record's** primary purpose is for documentation of clinical impressions and progress made in treatment.

- An essential part of the intake process is **data acquisition.**

- Income, educational attainment, gender, and religious affiliation are examples of **demographic data.**

- The concept of **entropy** is a part of General Systems Theory.

- The most widely used form of sampling, especially in experimental designs, is random sampling.

- Social work research constantly deals with issues of validity and reliability. In research it is not possible to have validity without reliability, but it is possible to have reliability without validity.

- The **modes of treatment** are family, community, group, couples, and individual

- **Person-centered therapy** is considered to be the most nondirective form of therapy.

- It is generally agreed that the best treatment for depression is action-oriented.

- **Feminist psychotherapy** is described as a philosophy of psychotherapy.

- To facilitate communication it is best to begin by attending to the client's feelings.

- In treating depression with behavioral therapy, the focus of the therapist is on specific observable behaviors.

- **Marriage and family therapy** can be said to be divided into two schools: the historical perspective and the interactional perspective.

- According to modern management philosophy, an appropriate role for an agency administrator is to implement policy.

- In working with clients we can help them to define their traits differently, using a technique called **reframing**. For instance, "lazy" can become "laid back," "mellow," "relaxed," "taking it easy."

- Five percent of the population age 65 and over suffers from **dementia** that interferes with cognitive functioning.

- The type of maltreatment of children most often reported is neglect.

- The I.Q. level of retardation generally referred to as "educable" is 50-55.

- Between six and twelve million children live in families with at least one alcoholic parent.

- A simple technique that a Social Worker can use to continue to grow in his/her ability to help is to focus on successes in order to repeat them.

- Language problems, illiteracy, economics, and cultural values create barriers to minorities' use of services.

- The major function of social work research is to assist in the development of knowledge.

- **Empowerment practice** focuses on issues of developing critical awareness and developing skills for change.

- The most important activity of the initial phase of conducting a research project is **problem selection**.

- **Depression in the elderly** can be masked by somatized complaints.

- Crisis and change have long been recognized as important in the emotional life of individuals and families.

- During the last twenty years **empowerment practice** has emerged in human services. The goal of this practice can be described as interventions directed to address the role of powerlessness in personal and social relationships.

- Psychological testing is not a major element of social work practice.

- Current estimates of alcoholism among the elderly are in the range of 2%.

- The Hispanic community is heterogenous.

- **Denial** best describes an individual who is not willing to admit that the death of his mother, whom he loved, was a painful and anxiety-producing event.

- **Empowerment of clients** includes exchanging information, consciousness-raising process, and requiring decision making.

- **Assessment skills** in social work are important, especially in the collection of relevant data.

- **Secondary alcoholism** includes individuals who are experiencing major psychiatric disorders before the onset of drinking problems.

- Twenty percent of **lithium patients** develop thyroid abnormalities.

- A major tenet of **role theory** is that the real-life behavior which it studies is determined socially.

- It is common practice within the social work profession to document clinical activities, administrative activities, and progress in the **case record**.

- The research design most effective in the generalization of findings due to methodological controls such as randomization and control groups is **experimental design**.

- A major component of the social work profession is **advocating for social justice**.

- **Supervision, training, and orientation of staff to agency mission, objectives, and goals** is becoming a common practice within many social work agencies.

- The primary function of the **research review committee** is to ensure that subjects are not adversely affected by the research.

- In most cases clinical treatment contracting is not an aspect of aftercare.

- **Randomization of groups** into experimental and control groups is a fundamental function of experimental research design.

- **Self-determinism** maintains that clients have a right to make their own decisions and manage their own affairs.

- **Personal identity** is influenced by many factors during the life cycle. The greatest influence on adolescent identity is often peer pressure.

- Although the **Americans with Disabilities Act** has been in effect for some time, the Equal Employment Opportunity Commission has only recently provided guidance to employers of workers with psychiatric disabilities.

- Attributing an unacceptable aspect of one's own personality to another person or entity is known as **projection**.

- Sigmund Freud made the most extensive use of **free association**.

- **Preventive mental health strategies** attempt to reduce the incidence of psychological disorders by establishing programs to alleviate poverty and other demoralizing situations.

- Empathetic understanding of the client's view of reality is a major goal of a Clinical Social Worker using **person-centered therapies**.

- Clinical Social Workers utilizing **Gestalt therapy** would be most likely to encourage clients to express their own moment-to-moment feelings.

- In classical conditioning therapies, maladaptive symptoms are considered to be **conditioned responses**.

■ The construction of an anxiety hierarchy and training in relaxation are important aspects of *systematic desensitization*.

Ventajas LLC.

Product Sales/Order Form

Date of Sale/Order ____ / ____ / ____

Name:_____	Phone Day: ____ / ____
Street/POB_____	Phone Eve: ____ / ____
City:_____	FAX: ____ / ____
State:_____ Zip Code:_____	e-mail:_____

Product	Price	Qty	Total
EXAMINATION PREMIER PACKAGE:			
Basic	$208.75	_____	
Intermediate	$225.75	_____	
Clinical	$238.50	_____	
ASSESSMENT:			
Basic	$60.50	_____	
Intermediate	$85.50	_____	
Clinical	$85.50	_____	
PRACTICE EXAMINATION (Q & A):			
Basic	$60.00	_____	
Intermediate	$65.50	_____	
Clinical	$70.50	_____	
Comprehensive	$60.50	_____	
Research	$60.50	_____	
STUDY MANUALS			
Basic	$167.00	_____	
Intermediate	$177.50	_____	
Clinical	$182.50	_____	
TEXTS:			
Social Work Memory Bites	$28.50	_____	
The Recovery Medicine Wheel	$28.50	_____	
EXAM PREPARATION SEMINAR	$ 275.50	_____	
POLO AND T-SHIRT			
Navy Poly Shirt - 100 year logo (Size One-size)	$25.00	_____	
White T-Shirt (Size ☐ M ☐Kid Size ☐ Large)	$18.50	_____	
White T-Shirt - Kids logo in teal (One size Adult)	$23.50	_____	
White T-Shirt - Freud in the Field (One Size Adult)	$23.50	_____	
Subtotal			
Total of Order			

Paid by: ☐Cash   ☐ Check#_____
☐MasterCard   ☐Visa

__ __ __ __ __ __ __ __ __ __ __ __ __ __ __ __
Exp:____ / ____
Signature:_____

Mail Product Sales/Order Form to: Ventajas, LLC, 6547 Sperryvile Pike, Boston, VA 22713
or
Give to a Ventajas Representative